Tolley

Authors: Alan Dolton MA (Oxon) and
Nicholas Bowen Barrister
Designer: Jonathan Newdick

Published by Tolley Publishing Co. Ltd,
2 Addiscombe Road, Croydon, Surrey CR9 5AF

© Tolley Publishing Company Limited 1990
A United Newspapers Publication

Typeset in Plantin by Kerrypress Ltd, Luton, Beds.
and printed by Penshurst Press Ltd.,
Tunbridge Wells, Kent.

ISBN 0 85459 455-8

Tax data 1990–91

Finance Bill 1990 Edition

About this book

This is the tenth edition of Tolley's Tax Data—a compendium of essential factual information for the tax adviser, covering all the main UK taxes and related matters. It includes the provisions of the 1990 Finance Bill and further important information up to 30 April 1990.

Comparative figures for up to six years are included in many of the tables.

Statutory references are also given.

Comments on this annual publication and suggestions for new material and improvements will always be welcome.

Subscribers who place a standing order for the book will receive a free half-yearly update (to be published in December 1990).

TOLLEY PUBLISHING CO. LTD.

Abbreviations

ACT	=	Advance Corporation Tax
CAA	=	Capital Allowances Act
CGTA	=	Capital Gains Tax Act
Conv	=	Convertible
CTTA	=	Capital Transfer Tax Act
Cum	=	Cumulative
FA	=	Finance Act
FB	=	Finance Bill
ICTA	=	Income and Corporation Taxes Act
IHTA	=	Inheritance Tax Act
IR	=	Inland Revenue
IRPR	=	Inland Revenue Press Release
ITA	=	Income Tax Act
Ord	=	Ordinary
PAYE	=	Pay as you earn
PET	=	Potentially exempt transfer
Pt	=	Part
s	=	Section
Sch	=	Schedule
SI	=	Statutory Instrument
SR & O	=	Statutory Rules and Orders
Stk	=	Stock
TMA	=	Taxes Management Act
VATA	=	Value Added Tax Act
WDV	=	Written Down Value

AA motoring costs

CROSS REFERENCES. Car benefit scale rates; Car fuel scale rates

Estimated motoring costs 1989—Petrol cars

Engine capacity (cc)	Up to 1,000	1,001 to 1,400	1,401 to 2,000	2,001 to 3,000	3,001 to 4,500
Standing charges per annum (£)					
(a) Car licence	100.00	100.00	100.00	100.00	100.00
(b) Insurance	449.44	550.88	647.79	1,045.98	1,176.33
(c) Depreciation	771.06	1,118.44	1,441.02	2,818.44	3,771.12
(d) Subscription	51.00	51.00	51.00	51.00	51.00
Total	1,371.50	1,820.32	2,239.81	4,015.42	5,098.45
Standing charges per mile (pence)					
5,000	27.430	36.406	44.796	80.308	101.968
10,000	13.715	18.203	22.398	40.154	50.984
15,000	10.171	13.627	16.853	30.527	39.018
20,000	9.171	12.457	15.522	28.532	36.806
25,000	8.570	11.755	14.723	27.335	35.478
30,000	7.142	9.796	12.269	22.779	29.565
Running costs per mile (pence)					
(e) Petrol**	4.600	5.257	6.134	8.364	9.200
(f) Oil	0.457	0.457	0.487	0.537	0.878
(g) Tyres	0.467	0.600	0.725	1.403	1.819
(h) Servicing	0.969	0.969	0.969	1.264	1.887
(i) Repairs and replacements	4.946	5.236	6.119	9.259	11.507
Total	11.439	12.519	14.434	20.827	25.291

★ Letters refer to notes
★★ At £1.84 per gallon (40.5p per litre) every penny more or less add or subtract:

	Up to 1,000	1,001 to 1,400	1,401 to 2,000	2,001 to 3,000	3,001 to 4,500
add or subtract:	0.025	0.028	0.033	0.045	0.050

Engine capacity (cc)	Up to 1,000	1,001 to 1,400	1,401 to 2,000	2,001 to 3,000	3,001 to 4,500
Total cost per mile (based on 10,000 miles) (pence)					
Standing charges	13.715	18.203	22.398	40.154	50.984
Running costs	11.439	12.519	14.434	20.827	25.291
Total	25.154	30.722	36.832	60.981	76.275

Previous years

Total cost per mile (based on 10,000 miles) (pence) (note j)	Up to 1,000	1,001 to 1,400	1,401 to 2,000	2,001 to 3,000	3,001 to 4,500
1989	23.633	28.854	34.241	56.777	71.408
1988	23.194	27.684	32.858	54.745	69.644
1987	28.260	33.927	40.070	65.858	84.782
1986	26.353	31.077	37.193	59.351	74.613
1985	25.692	29.642	35.355	56.292	71.965
1984	22.587	26.368	31.425	48.508	62.975
1983	21.176	24.991	29.904	45.479	60.656
1982	20.795	24.209	29.003	43.103	60.842

Notes

These figures are averages and actual figures should be substituted where possible

(a) **Car licence.** £100.00 at present.
(b) **Insurance.** Average rates for fully comprehensive policies. No allowance is made for the no-claim discount.
(c) **Depreciation** is based on average car prices when new, a mileage of 10,000 p.a. and assuming an economical life of 80,000 miles or eight years. In the case of second-hand vehicles the depreciation should be assessed individually.
(d) **AA subscription.** £45.50 p.a.
(e) **Petrol.** £1.84 per gallon. See the table for adjustments. For 1990, leaded petrol is likely to be more expensive than unleaded, and the figure of £1.84 per gallon is based on the anticipated price of unleaded petrol.
(f) **Engine oil.** Allowance is made for normal oil consumption and routine oil changes.
(g) **Tyres.** Estimated life of 30,000 miles.
(h) **Servicing.** Routine servicing as recommended by the manufacturers. In the case of older cars, servicing costs may be more.
(i) **Repairs and replacements.** Estimated on a basis of total cost of repairs, replacements and renovations over eight years or 80,000 miles.
(j) Before 1988, the AA included a figure for the loss of interest on capital used to purchase a car and a nominal amount for garage/parking. These figures were no longer included for 1988 and, therefore, figures for 1987 and earlier years do not invite direct comparison with those for 1988 to 1990.

Reprinted by kind permission of the Automobile Association.

1

Benefits in kind

CROSS REFERENCES. Car benefit scale rates; Car fuel scale rates

Benefit provided	Directors, and 'P11D' employees (see notes)	'Lower-paid' employees	Reference
Assets given to employees	If new, cost to employer If used, market value at time of transfer, or (if the asset, not being a car, first applied for the provision of a benefit after 5 April 1980 and a person has been chargeable to tax on its use) market value when first so applied less amounts charged to tax, if greater	Second-hand value	*ICTA 1988, s 156(1)* *ICTA 1988, s 156(3)(4)(9)*
Beneficial loans (a) Interest free or beneficial rates	Difference between interest paid and that payable at 'official rate'. No assessment where difference under £200 Official rate 16.5% p.a. after 5 Nov. 1989 15.5% p.a. after 5 July 1989 and before 6 Nov. 1989 14.5% p.a. after 5 Jan. 1989 and before 6 July 1989 13.5% p.a. after 5 Oct. 1988 and before 6 Jan. 1989 12% p.a. after 5 Aug. 1988 and before 6 Oct. 1988 9.5% p.a. after 5 May 1988 and before 6 Aug. 1988 10.5% p.a. after 5 Dec. 1987 and before 6 May 1988 11.5% p.a. after 5 Sept. 1987 and before 6 Dec. 1987 10.5% p.a. after 5 June 1987 and before 6 Sept. 1987 11.5% p.a. after 5 April 1987 and before 6 June 1987 12% p.a. after 5 Oct. 1982 and before 6 April 1987	Not taxable	 *IR Order, 20.10.1989* *SI 1989, No 1001* *SI 1988, No 2186* *SI 1988, No 1622* *SI 1988, No 1279* *SI 1988, No 757* *SI 1987, No 1989* *SI 1987, No 1493* *SI 1987, No 886* *SI 1987, No 512* *SI 1982, No 1273*
(b) Waiver	Amount written off	Normally taxable	*ICTA 1988, ss 160, 161*
Car parking spaces at or near place of work	Not taxable after 5 April 1988	Not taxable after 5 April 1988	*FA 1988, s 46*
Christmas parties etc.	Not taxable if 'modest' (currently £50 per head p.a.) and open to staff generally	Not taxable	*IRPR 20.10.88*
Company cars and car fuel (see pages 14 to 16)			
Credit tokens (1982/83 onwards)	Cost to employer of money, goods or services obtained less any contribution from employee	As aside	*ICTA 1988, s 142*
Living accommodation (a) Representative	Employees—no liability Directors—annual value or actual rent if greater (unless occupied for security purposes)	Not taxable	
(b) Beneficial	Annual value or actual rent if greater 1984/85 onwards—additional charge at annual rate equivalent to excess of cost of providing accommodation over £75,000 at official rate (see above), less net benefit under *ICTA 1988, s 145*	As aside	*ICTA 1988, s 145* *ICTA 1988, s 146*

Benefits in kind (continued)

Benefit provided	Directors, and 'P11D' employees (see notes)	'Lower-paid' employees	Reference
Living expenses (heating, lighting etc. borne by employer) (a) Company's accommodation			
(i) Representative	Cost to company subject to a maximum of 10% of net emoluments	Normally not taxable	*ICTA 1988, s 163*
(ii) Beneficial	Normally cost to employer	Normally not taxable	
(b) Own accommodation	Normally cost to employer	Normally as aside	
Long service awards	Not taxable provided at least 20 years' service and cost to employer does not exceed £20 (£10 before 13.3.84) for each year of service. No similar award must have been made in the previous 10 years	As aside	*IR1 (1988), A22*
Medical insurance	1982/83 onwards—premium paid on behalf of employee unless for treatment outside UK whilst employee performing his duties abroad	1982/83 onwards— not taxable	*ICTA 1988, s 155(6)*
Relocation expenses	Reasonable reimbursement not taxable NB: Contributions by employers to the extra costs incurred by employees moved to higher cost housing areas are, subject to certain conditions, non-taxable to the extent that they do not exceed the maximum amount payable in the Civil Service. The maximum after 31 May 1987 is For moves after 31 May 1987 and before 30 March 1988 £17,220 For moves after 29 March 1988 and before 1 October 1988 £15,750 For moves after 30 September 1988 and before 1 February 1989 £20,160 For moves after 31 January 1989 and before 1 December 1989 £21,210 For moves after 30 November 1989 and before 6 April 1990 £22,890 For moves after 5 April 1990 £24,150	As aside	*IR1 (1988), A5(a)* *IRPR 28.11.87* *IRPR 30.3.88* *IRPR 8.11.88* *IRPR 22.2.89* *IRPR 27.11.89* *IRPR 9.4.90*
Scholarships (awarded after 14 March 1983 to member of employee's family)	Cost of any scholarship awarded (i) out of a trust fund etc. not satisfying a 25% distribution test; or (ii) because of employee's employment	Not taxable	*ICTA 1988, s 165*
Use of employer's assets (other than cars)	Land at annual value; other assets at 20% of market value when first lent or rental charge if higher	Not taxable	*ICTA 1988, s 156(5)-(7)*
Vouchers			
(a) Cash vouchers	Cashable value	Cashable value	*ICTA 1988, s 143*
(b) Non-cash vouchers	Cost to employer less any contribution from employee	Cost to employer	*ICTA 1988, s 141*
(c) Luncheon vouchers	Excess over 15p per working day	As aside	*IR1 (1988), A2*
(d) Transport vouchers (1982/83 onwards)	Cost to employer less any contribution from employee	As aside (note c)	*ICTA 1988, s 141*
Workplace nurseries	Not taxable after 5 April 1990	Not taxable	*FB 1990*

Notes

(a) 'P11D' employees are those with emoluments, plus benefits etc. to be entered on form P11D (including VAT), at rate of £8,500 p.a. or more.

(b) 'Directors' exclude those with less than a 5% interest in the company provided that they are full-time working directors or the organisation is non-profit-making.

(c) Transport vouchers provided for 'lower-paid' employees of passenger transport undertakings under arrangements in operation on 25 March 1982 are not taxable. [*ICTA 1988, s 141(6)*].

Capital allowances

Expenditure after	Allowance	Reference
Agricultural and forestry land and buildings		
Initial allowance		
11 April 1978	20%	*CAA 1968, s 68(1)*
		as amended by
		FA 1978, s 39(1)
31 March 1986	Nil	*FA 1986, s 56, 15 Sch*
Writing-down allowance (on cost)		
5 April 1946	10%	*CAA 1968, s 68*
31 March 1986	4%	*CAA 1990, s 123*

Note

(a) Maximum allowance for farmhouse is on one third of expenditure. *CAA 1990, s 124(1)*

Cemeteries and crematoria

Start of base period for year 1954/55	(i) Cost of land (including levelling, draining etc.) sold for interments or memorial garden plots	*FA 1954, s 22*
		ICTA 1988, s 91

(ii) A proportion of residual capital expenditure at the end of the period in respect of eligible buildings, structures and land taken up calculated as follows

$$\text{Residual Capital Expenditure} \times \frac{A}{A + B}$$

where

A = number of grave spaces/garden plots sold in period
B = number of grave spaces/garden plots still available

Expenditure after	Allowance	Reference
Dredging		
Initial allowance		
5 April 1956	10%	*FA 1956, s 17(1)(a)*
14 April 1958	15%	*FA 1958, s 15(4)*
7 April 1959	5%	*FA 1959, s 21(4)*
	15% (where no investment allowance)	
16 January 1966	15%	*CAA 1968, s 67(1)(a)*
31 March 1968	Nil	*FA 1985, s 61*
Writing-down allowance (on cost)		
5 April 1905	2% from 1956/57 onwards	*FA 1956, s 17(1)(b)*
5 November 1962	4%	*CAA 1990, s 134(1)*
Dwelling-houses let on assured tenancies		
Initial allowance		
9 March 1982	75%	*FA 1982, 12 Sch (1)(2)*
13 March 1984	50%	
31 March 1985	25%	
31 March 1986	Nil	*FA 1984, s 58, 12 Sch 3*
Writing-down allowance (on cost)		
After 9 March 1982 and before 1 April 1992	4%	*CAA 1990, s 85*

Notes

(a) Maximum qualifying expenditure is £60,000 on a construction in Greater London and £40,000 elsewhere. *CAA 1990, s 96(1)*

(b) See note (b) on page 6 which also applies to initial allowances on assured tenancies.

(c) Before 15 March 1988, allowances were available only on qualifying expenditure on dwelling-houses on assured tenancies within the meaning of *Housing Act 1980, s 56*. Since the coming into force of *Housing Act 1988*, expenditure qualifies for allowances only in the following circumstances:

(i) if incurred or contracted for before 15 March 1988, either by an approved company (a company which on 15 March 1988 was an approved body under *Housing Act 1980, s 56(4)*) or by a person who sells the relevant interest to such a company before any of the dwelling-houses comprised in it are used; or

(ii) if incurred before 1 April 1992 by an approved company which, before 15 March 1988, bought or contracted to buy the relevant interest;

and then only if the tenancy in question, whenever created, is, for the purposes of *Housing Act 1988*, an assured tenancy other than an assured shorthold tenancy. *CAA 1990, s 84*

Capital allowances (continued)

Expenditure after	Allowance	Reference
Hotels (see note (a))		
Initial allowance		
11 April 1978	20%	FA 1978, 6 Sch 1
31 March 1986	Nil	FA 1985, s 66
Writing-down allowance (on cost)		
11 April 1978	4%	CAA 1990, s 19
Industrial buildings and sports pavilions		
Initial allowance		
5 April 1944	10%	ITA 1945, s 1
5 April 1952	Nil	FA 1951, s 20(1)
		ITA 1952, s 265
14 April 1953	10%	FA 1953, s 16(2)
6 April 1954	Nil	FA 1954, s 16(2)
	10% (where no investment allowance)	
17 February 1956	10%	FA 1956, s 15
14 April 1958	15%	FA 1958, s 15(1)(5)
7 April 1959	5%	FA 1959, s 21(1)(2), 4 Sch
	15% (where no investment allowance)	
16 January 1966	15%	FA 1966, s 35
5 April 1970	30%	
	40% (if in development or intermediate area or NI)	FA 1970, s 15(1)
21 March 1972	40%	FA 1972, s 67(2)(d)
12 November 1974	50%	FA 1975, s 13
10 March 1981	75%	FA 1981, s 73
13 March 1984	50%	
31 March 1985	25%	
31 March 1986	Nil	FA 1984, s 58, 12 Sch 1

Expenditure after	Allowance	Reference
Industrial buildings and sports pavilions (continued)		
Writing-down allowance (on cost)		
5 April 1946	2%	ITA 1945, s 2
		ITA 1952, s 266(1)
		CAA 1968, s 2(2)
5 November 1962	4%	CAA 1990, s 3

Notes

(a) An initial allowance of 100% is given on expenditure incurred or contracted for within ten years of the inclusion of the site (including a hotel) in an enterprise zone. — *CAA 1990, s 1(1)*

(b) An initial allowance of 100% was given for expenditure incurred on 'small workshops' (internal floor space 2,500 square feet or less) after 26 March 1980 and before 27 March 1983. — *FA 1980, s 75, 13 Sch*

(c) An initial allowance of 100% was given for expenditure incurred after 26 March 1983 and before 27 March 1985 on 'very small workshops' i.e. units not exceeding 1,250 square feet or which, in a converted building, exceed that area but where the average size of all units in the building does not exceed 1,250 square feet. — *FA 1982, s 73 / FA 1983, s 31*

(d) Where the allowances in (a) and (c) above are disclaimed or reduced, a writing-down allowance of 25% on cost is given. — *FA 1980, ss 74, 75, 13 Sch*

(e) See note (b) on page 6 which also applies to initial allowances on industrial buildings etc.

Know-how

Expenditure after	Allowance	Reference
Writing-down allowance		
19 March 1968	1/6th expenditure per annum	ICTA 1988, s 530(6)
31 March 1986	25% (on tax wdv)	ICTA 1988, s 530(2)

Capital allowances (continued)

Expenditure after	Allowance	Reference
Machinery and plant		
Initial allowance		
5 April 1944	20%	*ITA 1945, s 15*
5 April 1949	40%	*FA 1949, s 20*
5 April 1952	Nil	*ITA 1952, s 279*
14 April 1953	20%	*FA 1953, s 16*
6 April 1954	Nil	*FA 1954, s 16*
	20% (where no investment allowance)	
17 February 1956	20%	*FA 1956, s 15*
14 April 1958	30%	*FA 1958, s 15*
7 April 1959	10%	*FA 1959, s 21*
	30% (where no investment allowance)	
16 January 1966	30%	*FA 1966, s 35*
26 October 1970	Nil	*FA 1971, s 42*
First-year allowances (general)		
26 October 1970	60%	*FA 1971, s 42*
19 July 1971	80%	*FA 1972, s 67(1)(a)*
21 March 1972	100%	*FA 1972, s 67(2)(a)*
13 March 1984	75%	*FA 1984, s 58, 12 Sch 2*
31 March 1985	50%	
31 March 1986	Nil	

Expenditure after	Allowance	Reference
Machinery and plant (continued)		
Writing-down allowance (on tax wdv)		
6 April 1946	Various rates	
5 November 1962	Various rates	*CAA 1968, ss 19–22, 4 Sch*
26 October 1970	25%	*FA 1971, s 44(2)*
		CAA 1990, s 24(2)
Foreign leased assets		
After 9 March 1982	10%	*FA 1982, s 70*
		CAA 1990, s 42

Notes

(a) The reductions in rates from 13 March 1984 onwards do not apply to certain expenditure qualifying for regional development grants on projects in NI or which (on 13 March 1984) were in development areas, where the written offer of assistance was made after 31 March 1980 and before 14 March 1984.   *FA 1984, s 58, 12 Sch 4*

(b) Where a contract is made after 13 March 1984 and before 31 March 1986, and the completion date is after 31 March 1985 or is unspecified, then in respect of capital expenditure incurred in the years ended 31 March 1985 and 31 March 1986, the amount which attracts first-year allowances under the revised scales is limited to the part of the contract price falling in that year. The contract price is for this purpose apportioned evenly over the period from the contract date to the completion date (or to 31 March 1987 if earlier or no completion date is specified), complete months only being counted. The part of that period falling in a financial year is similarly by reference to complete months only. Any excess of actual expenditure over maximum allowable expenditure is treated as incurred in the following financial year. This anti-avoidance provision does not apply to expenditure on machinery or plant under a hire purchase or similar agreement.   *FA 1984, s 58, 12 Sch 5–7*

Capital allowances (continued)

Expenditure after	Allowance	Reference
Mines and oil wells		
Initial allowance		
5 April 1944	10%	*ITA 1945, s 26*
5 April 1952	Nil	*ITA 1952, s 306*
14 April 1953	40%	*FA 1953, s 16(3)*
6 April 1954	Nil	*FA 1954, s 16(4)*
	40% (where no investment allowance)	
17 February 1956	40%	*FA 1956, s 15(1)*
7 April 1959	20%	*FA 1959, s 21(2)*
	40% (where no investment allowance)	
16 January 1966	40%	*FA 1966, s 35*
		CAA 1968, s 56(2)
31 March 1986	Nil	*FA 1986, s 55, 13, 14 Schs*

Note

An allowance of 100% was given on expenditure incurred after 26 October 1970 and before 1 April 1986 on the construction of works in a development area or in Northern Ireland. *FA 1971, s 52*

Expenditure after	Allowance	Reference
Writing-down allowance		
Before 1 April 1986	Residue of expenditure × $\dfrac{A}{A+B}$ (subject to a minimum of 5% of residue of expenditure) where A = current output B = potential future output	*CAA 1968, s 57*
After 31 March 1986	25% (on tax wdv) 10% on minerals and mineral rights	*FA 1986, s 55, 13, 14 Schs* *CAA 1990, s 98(5)*

Note

After 31 March 1986, relief for land is abolished. Allowances are due on the residue of unrelieved expenditure incurred before 1 April 1986. As a transitional measure taxpayers have the option for one year to claim initial allowances for expenditure under a contract entered into before 16 July 1985. *FA 1986, s 55, 13, 14 Schs*

Expenditure after	Allowance	Reference
Motor cars suitable for private use		
Not eligible for initial allowance		
Writing-down allowance (on tax wdv)		
26 October 1970	25% (maximum £1,000)	*FA 1971, 8 Sch 10*
6 April 1976	25% (maximum £1,250)	*FA 1976, s 43(1)*
12 June 1979	25% (maximum £2,000)	*F(No 2)A 1979, s 14(5)* *CAA 1990, ss 34, 35*
Patent rights		
Writing-down allowance		
5 April 1946 (or 8 July 1952 for right to acquire future patent rights)	Expenditure on purchase in equal instalments over 17 years; or if shorter, period for which rights acquired; or if shorter, 17 years less the number of complete years between the start of the patent and the date of purchase, with a minimum of one year	*ICTA 1988, s 522*
31 March 1986	25% (on tax wdv)	*ICTA 1988, s 520*
Scientific research		
Allowance in year 1		
5 April 1946	20%	*FA 1944, s 28(1)* *F(No 2)A 1945, s 18*
5 April 1949	60%	*FA 1949, s 20(2)*
5 November 1962	100%	*FA 1963, s 36* *CAA 1968, s 91* *CAA 1990, s 137*
Allowance in years 2–5 (inclusive)		
5 April 1946	20%	*FA 1944, s 28(1)* *F(No 2)A 1945, s 18*
5 April 1949	10%	*FA 1949, s 20(2)*
5 November 1962	Nil	*FA 1963, s 36*

Capital gains tax rates, reliefs and lease depreciation table

CROSS REFERENCES. Government securities; Interest on overdue tax; Negligible value securities; Payment of tax; Retail price index

Rates

After 5 April 1988, gains are chargeable to capital gains tax
(a) for individuals, at the rates that would apply if they were the top slice of income;
(b) for discretionary and accumulation trusts, at a rate equivalent to the total of the basic and additional rates of income tax (35% for 1988/89 to 1990/91);
(c) for other trusts and for personal representatives, at a rate equivalent to the basic rate of income tax (25% for 1988/89 to 1990/91). *FA 1988, ss 98, 100*
Before 6 April 1988, the rate of capital gains tax was 30%. *CGTA 1979, s 3*

Relief for small gains

(a) Individuals, personal representatives for the year of death and following two years and trusts for mentally disabled or those in receipt of an attendance allowance

1988/89 to 1990/91	£5,000 or less—Nil	FA 1988, s 108
1987/88	£6,600 or less—Nil	SI 1987, No 436
1986/87	£6,300 or less—Nil	SI 1986, No 527
1985/86	£5,900 or less—Nil	SI 1985, No 428
1984/85	£5,600 or less—Nil	SI 1984, No 343
1983/84	£5,300 or less—Nil	SI 1983, No 402

From 1981/82 onwards, in respect of qualifying trusts above, where one person creates more than one settlement, the exemption above is divided by the number of settlements created after 9 March 1981, subject to a minimum of 10% of the annual exemption *FA 1982, s 80* *FA 1981, s 89*

(b) Settlements other than trusts covered in (a) above

1988/89 to 1990/91	£2,500 or less—Nil	CGTA 1979, 1 Sch 6(2)
1987/88	£3,300 or less—Nil	SI 1987, No 436
1986/87	£3,150 or less—Nil	SI 1986, No 527
1985/86	£2,950 or less—Nil	SI 1985, No 428
1984/85	£2,800 or less—Nil	SI 1984, No 343
1983/84	£2,650 or less—Nil	SI 1983, No 402

From 1980/81 onwards, in respect of settlements made after 6 June 1978, where one person creates more than one settlement, the exemption above is divided by the number of settlements created, subject to a minimum of 10% of the annual exemption for individuals *FA 1982, s 80* *CGTA 1979, 1 Sch 6(4)* *FA 1980, s 78(3)(4)*

Lease depreciation table

This table relates to leases of land which have 50 years or less to run (short leases)

Years	Percentage	Years	Percentage	Years	Percentage
50 or more	100	33	90.280	16	64.116
49	99.657	32	89.354	15	61.617
48	99.289	31	88.371	14	58.971
47	98.902	30	87.330	13	56.167
46	98.490	29	86.226	12	53.191
45	98.059	28	85.053	11	50.038
44	97.595	27	83.816	10	46.695
43	97.107	26	82.496	9	43.154
42	96.593	25	81.100	8	39.399
41	96.041	24	79.622	7	35.414
40	95.457	23	78.055	6	31.195
39	94.842	22	76.399	5	26.722
38	94.189	21	74.635	4	21.983
37	93.497	20	72.770	3	16.959
36	92.761	19	70.791	2	11.629
35	91.981	18	68.697	1	5.983
34	91.156	17	66.470	0	0

The fraction of expenditure (original cost and additional expenditure being treated separately) which is not allowed is calculated from the table above as follows

$$\frac{P(1)-P(3)}{P(1)} \quad \text{or} \quad \frac{P(2)-P(3)}{P(2)}$$

where the percentages for the duration of the lease are
P(1) at acquisition
P(2) at the time of any additional expenditure
P(3) at disposal

If the duration of the lease is not an exact number of years, the percentage shall be for the whole number of years plus one-twelfth of the difference between that and the next higher number for each odd month, counting an odd fourteen days or more as one month.
[CGTA 1979, 3 Sch 1(3)–(6)].

CROSS REFERENCES. Government securities; Interest on overdue tax; Negligible value securities; Payment of tax; Retail price index

Indexation

General rules

Gains and losses on disposals of assets are computed by deducting allowable expenditure from the amount realised (or deemed to be realised) on disposal. For disposals after 5 April 1982 (31 March 1982 for companies) an 'indexation allowance' is deducted. For disposals before 6 April 1985 (1 April 1985 for companies) the asset had to be held for twelve months to qualify for indexation. The indexation allowance is the aggregate of the indexed rise of each item of allowable expenditure and the indexed rise is computed by multiplying each item of allowable expenditure by

$$\frac{RD-RI}{RI}$$

where

RD = retail price index for the month in which disposal occurs

RI = retail price index for the later of March 1982 or the month expenditure is incurred (the twelfth month after expenditure is incurred for disposals before 6 April 1985 (1 April 1985 for companies))

See page 61 for appropriate values of the retail price index to substitute in the above fraction. See pages 10–17 for tables of indexation allowance.

Losses

The indexation allowance applies to losses as it applies to gains. Before 6 April 1985 (1 April 1985 for companies) there was no allowance where a loss arose and no loss could be created by an allowance.

Assets acquired before 1 April 1982

For disposals after 5 April 1985 (31 March 1985 for companies) and before 6 April 1988, a claim may be made for the indexation allowance due on an asset held on 31 March 1982 to be calculated by reference to its market value on that date rather than its cost. For disposals after 5 April 1988, this applies automatically without the need to claim, but the allowance can be claimed on the original cost if this is to the taxpayer's advantage.

[FA 1982, ss 86, 87, 13 Sch; FA 1985, s 68, 19 Sch; FA 1988, s 118]

Personal representatives

The Inland Revenue have agreed that expenditure based on the following scales may be added to the market values of assets at the date of death (as an estimate of the legal and accountancy costs in preparing the inheritance tax account and obtaining probate etc.) in computing chargeable gains on disposal

Gross value of estate	Allowable expenditure
(a) Up to £20,000	1.5% of probate value of assets sold
(b) £20,001–£30,000	£300—divided among all the assets in the estate in proportion to their probate values
(c) £30,001–£150,000	1% of probate value of assets sold
(d) £150,001–£200,000	£1,500—divided as in (b) above
(e) £200,001–£400,000	0.75% of probate value of assets sold
(f) Over £400,000	By negotiation with Inspector

(Inland Revenue Statement of Practice SP 7/81)

Retirement relief

The amount of the relief is a percentage of £125,000 (£100,000 before 6 April 1987 and after 5 April 1985) determined according to the length of the qualifying period. It rises from 10% where the period is precisely one year to 100% where it is ten years (with time apportionment for part of a year). For disposals after 5 April 1988, one half of eligible gains between £125,000 and £500,000 (these limits being proportionately reduced for qualifying periods of less than ten years) is also exempt. To qualify for retirement relief, the disponer must have reached the age of 60 or retired below that age on ill-health grounds. Before 6 April 1985, eligible gains were reduced by £20,000 (£10,000 before 6 April 1983) for each year by which the disponer's age exceeded 60 (with time apportionment for part of a year) up to a maximum of £100,000 (£50,000 before 6 April 1983). [CGTA 1979, s 124; FA 1984, s 63(4); FA 1985, ss 69, 70, 20 Sch; FA 1987, s 47; FA 1988, s 110]

Tangible moveable assets (other than currency)

Disposals of £6,000 or less for 1989/90 and 1990/91 (£3,000 or less for 1982/83 to 1988/89) are exempt with marginal relief limiting any gain to five-thirds of the excess. [CGTA 1979, s 128; FA 1982, s 81; FA 1989, s 123]

Rebasing after 5 April 1988

Gains and losses on disposals after 5 April 1988 of assets held on 31 March 1982 are computed by reference to their 31 March 1982 value rather than original cost. However, a gain or loss cannot be greater than would have been the case if the rules relating to pre-6 April 1988 disposals had applied, unless a once and for all election is made for 31 March 1982 value to apply to all assets held on that date. [FA 1988, ss 96, 97; IRPR 11.5.88]

Table of indexation allowances for 1988–89 disposals for capital gains tax purposes

Month of Disposal – percentage figures

Month of Acquisition	1988 April	May	June	July	August	September	October	November	December	1989 January	February	March	April
March 1982	33.2	33.7	34.2	34.3	35.8	36.5	37.8	38.5	38.8	39.7	40.7	41.4	43.9
April	30.6	31.0	31.5	31.7	33.1	33.8	35.1	35.7	36.1	37.0	38.0	38.6	41.0
May	29.6	30.1	30.6	30.7	32.2	32.8	34.2	34.8	35.1	36.0	37.0	37.6	40.0
June	29.3	29.7	30.2	30.4	31.8	32.4	33.8	34.4	34.8	35.6	36.6	37.2	39.6
July	29.2	29.7	30.2	30.3	31.8	32.4	33.7	34.3	34.7	35.6	36.5	37.2	39.6
August	29.2	29.7	30.2	30.3	31.7	32.4	33.7	34.3	34.7	35.5	36.5	37.1	39.6
September	29.3	29.7	30.2	30.4	31.8	32.4	33.8	34.4	34.8	35.6	36.6	37.2	39.6
October	28.6	29.1	29.6	29.7	31.2	31.8	33.1	33.7	34.1	34.9	35.9	36.5	39.0
November	28.0	28.5	29.0	29.1	30.5	31.1	32.5	33.1	33.4	34.3	35.3	35.9	38.3
December	28.2	28.7	29.2	29.3	30.8	31.4	32.7	33.3	33.7	34.5	35.5	36.1	38.5
January 1983	28.1	28.6	29.0	29.2	30.6	31.2	32.5	33.2	33.5	34.4	35.3	35.9	38.4
February	27.5	28.0	28.5	28.6	30.1	30.7	32.0	32.6	32.9	33.8	34.8	35.4	37.8
March	27.3	27.8	28.3	28.4	29.8	30.4	31.7	32.3	32.7	33.5	34.5	35.1	37.5
April	25.5	26.0	26.5	26.6	28.0	28.6	29.9	30.5	30.9	31.7	32.6	33.2	35.6
May	25.0	25.5	25.9	26.1	27.5	28.1	29.4	30.0	30.3	31.1	32.1	32.7	35.0
June	24.7	25.2	25.6	25.8	27.2	27.8	29.1	29.7	30.0	30.8	31.8	32.4	34.7
July	24.0	24.5	25.0	25.1	26.5	27.1	28.4	29.0	29.3	30.1	31.1	31.7	34.0
August	23.5	24.0	24.4	24.5	25.9	26.5	27.8	28.4	28.7	29.6	30.5	31.1	33.4
September	22.9	23.4	23.9	24.0	25.4	26.0	27.2	27.8	28.2	29.0	29.9	30.5	32.8
October	22.5	23.0	23.4	23.5	24.9	25.5	26.8	27.4	27.7	28.5	29.5	30.0	32.3
November	22.1	22.5	23.0	23.1	24.5	25.1	26.3	26.9	27.3	28.1	29.0	29.6	31.9
December	21.8	22.2	22.7	22.8	24.2	24.7	26.0	26.6	26.9	27.7	28.7	29.2	31.5

Table of indexation allowances for 1988–89 disposals for capital gains tax purposes

Month of Disposal – *percentage figures*

Month of Acquisition	1988 April	May	June	July	August	September	October	November	December	1989 January	February	March	April
January 1984	21.8	22.3	22.7	22.9	24.2	24.8	26.1	26.7	27.0	27.8	28.7	29.3	31.6
February	21.3	21.8	22.2	22.4	23.7	24.3	25.6	26.1	26.5	27.3	28.2	28.8	31.1
March	20.9	21.4	21.9	22.0	23.3	23.9	25.2	25.7	26.1	26.9	27.8	28.4	30.7
April	19.4	19.8	20.3	20.4	21.7	22.3	23.5	24.1	24.4	25.2	26.1	26.7	28.9
May	18.9	19.4	19.8	19.9	21.3	21.8	23.1	23.6	24.0	24.8	25.7	26.2	28.5
June	18.6	19.1	19.5	19.6	21.0	21.5	22.8	23.3	23.7	24.4	25.3	25.9	28.1
July	18.7	19.2	19.6	19.8	21.1	21.7	22.9	23.5	23.8	24.6	25.5	26.0	28.3
August	17.6	18.1	18.5	18.6	20.0	20.5	21.8	22.3	22.6	23.4	24.3	24.9	27.1
September	17.4	17.9	18.3	18.4	19.7	20.3	21.5	22.1	22.4	23.2	24.1	24.6	26.8
October	16.7	17.1	17.6	17.7	19.0	19.6	20.8	21.3	21.6	22.4	23.3	23.9	26.1
November	16.3	16.8	17.2	17.3	18.6	19.2	20.4	20.9	21.3	22.0	22.9	23.5	25.7
December	16.4	16.9	17.3	17.4	18.7	19.3	20.5	21.0	21.4	22.1	23.0	23.6	25.8
January 1985	16.0	16.4	16.9	17.0	18.3	18.9	20.1	20.6	20.9	21.7	22.6	23.1	25.3
February	15.1	15.5	15.9	16.1	17.4	17.9	19.1	19.6	20.0	20.7	21.6	22.1	24.3
March	14.0	14.4	14.9	15.0	16.3	16.8	18.0	18.5	18.9	19.6	20.5	21.0	23.2
April	11.6	12.1	12.5	12.6	13.8	14.4	15.5	16.1	16.4	17.1	18.0	18.5	20.6
May	11.1	11.5	12.0	12.1	13.3	13.9	15.0	15.5	15.9	16.6	17.4	18.0	20.1
June	10.9	11.3	11.7	11.8	13.1	13.6	14.8	15.3	15.6	16.3	17.2	17.7	19.8
July	11.1	11.5	11.9	12.0	13.3	13.8	15.0	15.5	15.8	16.6	17.4	17.9	20.0
August	10.8	11.2	11.6	11.7	13.0	13.5	14.7	15.2	15.5	16.2	17.1	17.6	19.7
September	10.9	11.3	11.7	11.8	13.1	13.6	14.7	15.3	15.6	16.3	17.1	17.7	19.8

Table of indexation allowances for 1988–89 disposals for capital gains tax purposes

Month of Disposal – percentage figures

Month of Acquisition	1988 April	May	June	July	August	September	October	November	December	1989 January	February	March	April
October 1985	10.7	11.1	11.5	11.6	12.9	13.4	14.6	15.1	15.4	16.1	17.0	17.5	19.6
November	10.3	10.7	11.1	11.2	12.5	13.0	14.2	14.7	15.0	15.7	16.6	17.1	19.2
December	10.2	10.6	11.0	11.1	12.3	12.9	14.0	14.5	14.8	15.6	16.4	16.9	19.0
January 1986	9.9	10.3	10.8	10.9	12.1	12.6	13.8	14.3	14.6	15.3	16.2	16.7	18.8
February	9.5	9.9	10.3	10.5	11.7	12.2	13.4	13.9	14.2	14.9	15.7	16.2	18.3
March	9.4	9.8	10.2	10.3	11.5	12.1	13.2	13.7	14.0	14.8	15.6	16.1	18.2
April	8.3	8.7	9.1	9.2	10.5	11.0	12.1	12.6	12.9	13.7	14.5	15.0	17.0
May	8.1	8.5	8.9	9.0	10.3	10.8	11.9	12.4	12.7	13.4	14.3	14.8	16.8
June	8.2	8.6	9.0	9.1	10.3	10.8	12.0	12.5	12.8	13.5	14.3	14.8	16.9
July	8.5	8.9	9.3	9.4	10.6	11.2	12.3	12.8	13.1	13.8	14.6	15.2	17.2
August	8.2	8.6	9.0	9.1	10.3	10.8	11.9	12.5	12.8	13.5	14.3	14.8	16.8
September	7.6	8.0	8.4	8.5	9.8	10.3	11.4	11.9	12.2	12.9	13.7	14.2	16.3
October	7.5	7.9	8.3	8.4	9.6	10.1	11.2	11.7	12.0	12.7	13.6	14.1	16.1
November	6.6	7.0	7.4	7.5	8.7	9.2	10.3	10.8	11.1	11.8	12.6	13.1	15.1
December	6.2	6.6	7.0	7.1	8.3	8.8	9.9	10.4	10.7	11.4	12.2	12.7	14.7
January 1987	5.8	6.2	6.6	6.7	7.9	8.4	9.5	10.3	10.3	11.0	11.8	12.3	14.3
February	5.4	5.8	6.2	6.3	7.5	8.0	9.1	9.6	9.9	10.6	11.4	11.9	13.8
March	5.2	5.6	6.0	6.1	7.3	7.8	8.8	9.3	9.6	10.3	11.1	11.6	13.6
April	3.9	4.3	4.7	4.8	6.0	6.5	7.6	8.1	8.3	9.0	9.8	10.3	12.3
May	3.8	4.2	4.6	4.7	5.9	6.4	7.5	7.9	8.2	8.9	9.7	10.2	12.2
June	3.8	4.2	4.6	4.7	5.9	6.4	7.5	7.9	8.2	8.9	9.7	10.2	12.2

Table of indexation allowances for 1988–89 disposals for capital gains tax purposes

Month of Disposal – percentage figures

Month of Acquisition	1988 April	May	June	July	August	September	October	November	December	1989 January	February	March	April
July 1987	3.9	4.3	4.7	4.8	6.0	6.5	7.6	8.1	8.3	9.0	9.8	10.3	12.3
August	3.6	4.0	4.4	4.5	5.7	6.2	7.2	7.7	8.0	8.7	9.5	10.0	11.9
September	3.3	3.7	4.1	4.2	5.4	5.9	6.9	7.4	7.7	8.4	9.2	9.7	11.6
October	2.8	3.2	3.6	3.7	4.9	5.3	6.4	6.9	7.2	7.9	8.6	9.1	11.1
November	2.3	2.7	3.1	3.2	4.4	4.8	5.9	6.4	6.7	7.4	8.1	8.6	10.5
December	2.4	2.8	3.2	3.3	4.5	4.9	6.0	6.5	6.8	7.5	8.2	8.7	10.6
January 1988	2.4	2.8	3.2	3.3	4.5	4.9	6.0	6.5	6.8	7.5	8.2	8.7	10.6
February	2.0	2.4	2.8	2.9	4.1	4.5	5.6	6.1	6.4	7.0	7.8	8.3	10.2
March	1.6	2.0	2.4	2.5	3.7	4.1	5.2	5.7	6.0	6.6	7.4	7.9	9.8
April		0.4	0.8	0.9	2.0	2.5	3.5	4.0	4.3	4.9	5.7	6.1	8.0
May			0.4	0.5	1.6	2.1	3.1	3.6	3.9	4.5	5.3	5.7	7.6
June				0.1	1.2	1.7	2.7	3.2	3.5	4.1	4.9	5.3	7.2
July					1.1	1.6	2.6	3.1	3.4	4.0	4.8	5.2	7.1
August						0.5	1.5	1.9	2.2	2.9	3.6	4.1	5.9
September							1.0	1.5	1.8	2.4	3.1	3.6	5.4
October								0.5	0.7	1.4	2.1	2.6	4.4
November									0.3	0.9	1.6	2.1	3.9
December										0.6	1.4	1.8	3.6
January 1989											0.7	1.2	3.0
February												0.4	2.2
March													1.8
April													

Table of indexation allowances for 1989–90 disposals for capital gains tax purposes

Month of Disposal – percentage figures

Month of Acquisition	1989 April	May	June	July	August	September	October	November	December	1990 January	February	March	April
March 1982	43.9	44.8	45.3	45.4	45.8	46.8	47.9	49.2	49.5	50.4	51.3	52.8	57.5
April	41.0	41.9	42.4	42.5	42.9	43.9	45.0	46.2	46.6	47.5	48.3	49.8	54.4
May	40.0	40.9	41.4	41.5	41.9	42.9	44.0	45.2	45.5	46.4	47.3	48.7	53.3
June	39.6	40.5	41.0	41.1	41.5	42.5	43.6	44.8	45.1	46.0	46.9	48.3	52.8
July	39.6	40.5	40.9	41.1	41.4	42.4	43.5	44.7	45.1	46.0	46.8	48.3	52.8
August	39.6	40.4	40.9	41.0	41.4	42.4	43.5	44.7	45.1	45.9	46.8	48.2	52.7
September	39.6	40.5	41.0	41.1	41.5	42.5	43.6	44.8	45.1	46.0	46.9	48.3	52.8
October	39.0	39.8	40.3	40.4	40.8	41.8	42.8	44.1	44.4	45.3	46.1	47.6	52.1
November	38.3	39.1	39.6	39.7	40.1	41.1	42.1	43.4	43.7	44.6	45.4	46.9	51.3
December	38.5	39.4	39.9	40.0	40.3	41.3	42.4	43.6	44.0	44.8	45.7	47.1	51.6
January 1983	38.4	39.2	39.7	39.8	40.2	41.1	42.2	43.4	43.8	44.7	45.5	47.0	51.4
February	37.8	38.6	39.1	39.2	39.6	40.5	41.6	42.8	43.2	44.0	44.9	46.3	50.8
March	37.5	38.4	38.8	39.0	39.3	40.3	41.4	42.6	42.9	43.8	44.6	46.1	50.5
April	35.6	36.4	36.9	37.0	37.4	38.3	39.4	40.6	41.0	41.8	42.6	44.0	48.4
May	35.0	35.9	36.3	36.5	36.8	37.8	38.8	40.0	40.4	41.2	42.0	43.4	47.8
June	34.7	35.5	36.0	36.1	36.5	37.4	38.5	39.7	40.0	40.9	41.7	43.1	47.5
July	34.0	34.8	35.3	35.4	35.8	36.7	37.8	38.9	39.3	40.1	40.9	42.3	46.7
August	33.4	34.2	34.7	34.8	35.2	36.1	37.1	38.3	38.7	39.5	40.3	41.7	46.0
September	32.8	33.6	34.1	34.2	34.6	35.5	36.5	37.7	38.0	38.9	39.7	41.1	45.4
October	32.3	33.2	33.6	33.7	34.1	35.0	36.1	37.2	37.6	38.4	39.2	40.6	44.9
November	31.9	32.7	33.2	33.3	33.6	34.5	35.6	36.7	37.1	37.9	38.7	40.1	44.3
December	31.5	32.3	32.8	32.9	33.3	34.2	35.2	36.4	36.7	37.5	38.3	39.7	44.0
January 1984	31.6	32.4	32.9	33.0	33.3	34.3	35.3	36.5	36.8	37.6	38.4	39.8	44.1
February	31.1	31.9	32.3	32.5	32.8	33.7	34.7	35.9	36.2	37.0	37.8	39.2	43.5

Table of indexation allowances for 1989–90 disposals for capital gains tax purposes

Month of Disposal – percentage figures

Month of Acquisition	1989 April	May	June	July	August	September	October	November	December	1990 January	February	March	April
March 1984	30.7	31.5	31.9	32.0	32.4	33.3	34.3	35.5	35.8	36.6	37.4	38.8	43.0
April	28.9	29.7	30.2	30.3	30.6	31.5	32.6	33.7	34.0	34.8	35.6	37.0	41.1
May	28.5	29.3	29.7	29.8	30.2	31.1	32.1	33.2	33.5	34.3	35.1	36.4	40.6
June	28.1	28.9	29.4	29.5	29.8	30.7	31.7	32.8	33.2	34.0	34.8	36.1	40.2
July	28.3	29.1	29.5	29.6	30.0	30.9	31.9	33.0	33.3	34.1	34.9	36.3	40.4
August	27.1	27.9	28.3	28.4	28.8	29.6	30.6	31.8	32.1	32.9	33.6	35.0	39.1
September	26.8	27.6	28.1	28.2	28.5	29.4	30.4	31.5	31.8	32.6	33.4	34.7	38.8
October	26.1	26.8	27.3	27.4	27.7	28.6	29.6	30.7	31.0	31.8	32.6	33.9	38.0
November	25.7	26.4	26.9	27.0	27.3	28.2	29.2	30.3	30.6	31.4	32.2	33.5	37.5
December	25.8	26.5	27.0	27.1	27.4	28.3	29.3	30.4	30.7	31.5	32.3	33.6	37.7
January 1985	25.3	26.1	26.5	26.6	27.0	27.8	28.8	29.9	30.3	31.0	31.8	33.1	37.2
February	24.3	25.1	25.5	25.6	26.0	26.8	27.8	28.9	29.2	30.0	30.7	32.0	36.1
March	23.2	23.9	24.4	24.5	24.8	25.6	26.6	27.7	28.0	28.8	29.5	30.8	34.8
April	20.6	21.3	21.8	21.9	22.2	23.0	24.0	25.0	25.3	26.1	26.8	28.1	32.0
May	20.1	20.8	21.2	21.3	21.6	22.5	23.4	24.5	24.8	25.5	26.2	27.5	31.4
June	19.8	20.5	20.9	21.1	21.4	22.2	23.2	24.2	24.5	25.2	26.0	27.2	31.1
July	20.0	20.8	21.2	21.3	21.6	22.4	23.4	24.4	24.7	25.5	26.2	27.5	31.4
August	19.7	20.4	20.9	21.0	21.3	22.1	23.1	24.1	24.4	25.1	25.9	27.1	31.0
September	19.8	20.5	20.9	21.0	21.3	22.2	23.1	24.2	24.5	25.2	25.9	27.2	31.1
October	19.6	20.3	20.7	20.8	21.1	22.0	22.9	24.0	24.3	25.0	25.7	27.0	30.9
November	19.2	19.9	20.3	20.4	20.7	21.6	22.5	23.5	23.9	24.6	25.3	26.6	30.4
December	19.0	19.7	20.2	20.3	20.6	21.4	22.3	23.4	23.7	24.4	25.1	26.4	30.3
January 1986	18.8	19.5	19.9	20.0	20.3	21.1	22.1	23.1	23.4	24.2	24.9	26.1	30.0
February	18.3	19.0	19.5	19.6	19.9	20.7	21.6	22.7	23.0	23.7	24.4	25.7	29.5

Table of indexation allowances for 1989–90 disposals for capital gains tax purposes

Month of Disposal – percentage figures

Month of Acquisition	1989 April	May	June	July	August	September	October	November	December	1990 January	February	March	April
March 1986	18.2	18.9	19.3	19.4	19.7	20.5	21.5	22.5	22.8	23.5	24.3	25.5	29.3
April	17.0	17.7	18.2	18.3	18.6	19.4	20.3	21.3	21.6	22.4	23.1	24.3	28.1
May	16.8	17.5	17.9	18.0	18.4	19.2	20.1	21.1	21.4	22.1	22.8	24.1	27.9
June	16.9	17.6	18.0	18.1	18.4	19.2	20.1	21.2	21.5	22.2	22.9	24.1	27.9
July	17.2	17.9	18.3	18.4	18.7	19.6	20.5	21.5	21.8	22.5	23.3	24.5	28.3
August	16.8	17.6	18.0	18.1	18.4	19.2	20.1	21.1	21.4	22.2	22.9	24.1	27.9
September	16.3	17.0	17.4	17.5	17.8	18.6	19.5	20.5	20.9	21.6	22.3	23.5	27.3
October	16.1	16.8	17.2	17.3	17.6	18.4	19.3	20.4	20.7	21.4	22.1	23.3	27.1
November	15.1	15.8	16.2	16.3	16.6	17.4	18.3	19.3	19.6	20.4	21.1	22.3	26.0
December	14.7	15.4	15.8	15.9	16.2	17.0	17.9	19.0	19.3	20.0	20.7	21.9	25.6
January 1987	14.3	15.0	15.4	15.5	15.8	16.6	17.5	18.5	18.8	19.5	20.2	21.4	25.1
February	13.8	14.5	14.9	15.0	15.3	16.1	17.0	18.0	18.3	19.0	19.7	20.9	24.6
March	13.6	14.3	14.7	14.8	15.1	15.9	16.8	17.8	18.1	18.8	19.5	20.7	24.4
April	12.3	13.0	13.4	13.5	13.8	14.5	15.4	16.4	16.7	17.4	18.1	19.3	22.9
May	12.2	12.9	13.2	13.3	13.6	14.4	15.3	16.3	16.6	17.3	18.0	19.1	22.8
June	12.2	12.9	13.2	13.3	13.6	14.4	15.3	16.3	16.6	17.3	18.0	19.1	22.8
July	12.3	13.0	13.4	13.5	13.8	14.5	15.4	16.4	16.7	17.4	18.1	19.3	22.9
August	11.9	12.6	13.0	13.1	13.4	14.2	15.1	16.1	16.4	17.0	17.7	18.9	22.5
September	11.6	12.3	12.7	12.8	13.1	13.9	14.7	15.7	16.0	16.7	17.4	18.6	22.2
October	11.1	11.8	12.1	12.2	12.5	13.3	14.2	15.2	15.5	16.1	16.8	18.0	21.6
November	10.5	11.2	11.6	11.7	12.0	12.8	13.6	14.6	14.9	15.6	16.2	17.4	21.0
December	10.6	11.3	11.7	11.8	12.1	12.9	13.7	14.7	15.0	15.7	16.4	17.5	21.1
January 1988	10.6	11.3	11.7	11.8	12.1	12.9	13.7	14.7	15.0	15.7	16.4	17.5	21.1
February	10.2	10.9	11.3	11.4	11.7	12.4	13.3	14.3	14.6	15.2	15.9	17.1	20.6

Table of indexation allowances for 1989–90 disposals for capital gains tax purposes

Month of Disposal – percentage figures

Month of Acquisition	1989 April	May	June	July	August	September	October	November	December	1990 January	February	March	April
March 1988	9.8	10.5	10.9	11.0	11.2	12.0	12.9	13.8	14.1	14.8	15.5	16.6	20.2
April	8.0	8.7	9.1	9.2	9.5	10.2	11.1	12.0	12.3	12.9	13.6	14.7	18.2
May	7.6	8.3	8.7	8.8	9.0	9.8	10.6	11.6	11.9	12.5	13.2	14.3	17.8
June	7.2	7.9	8.3	8.3	8.6	9.4	10.2	11.2	11.4	12.1	12.8	13.9	17.4
July	7.1	7.8	8.2	8.2	8.5	9.3	10.1	11.1	11.3	12.0	12.7	13.8	17.2
August	5.9	6.6	7.0	7.0	7.3	8.1	8.9	9.8	10.1	10.8	11.4	12.5	15.9
September	5.4	6.1	6.5	6.5	6.8	7.6	8.4	9.3	9.6	10.2	10.9	12.0	15.4
October	4.4	5.0	5.4	5.5	5.8	6.5	7.3	8.2	8.5	9.1	9.8	10.9	14.2
November	3.9	4.5	4.9	5.0	5.3	6.0	6.8	7.7	8.0	8.6	9.3	10.4	13.7
December	3.6	4.3	4.6	4.7	5.0	5.7	6.5	7.4	7.7	8.3	9.0	10.1	13.4
January 1989	3.0	3.6	4.0	4.1	4.3	5.0	5.9	6.8	7.0	7.7	8.3	9.4	12.7
February	2.2	2.9	3.2	3.3	3.6	4.3	5.1	6.0	6.3	6.9	7.5	8.6	11.9
March	1.8	2.4	2.8	2.8	3.1	3.8	4.6	5.5	5.8	6.4	7.0	8.1	11.4
April		0.6	1.0	1.0	1.3	2.0	2.8	3.7	3.9	4.5	5.2	6.2	9.4
May			0.3	0.4	0.7	1.4	2.2	3.0	3.3	3.9	4.5	5.6	8.8
June				0.1	0.3	1.0	1.8	2.7	2.9	3.6	4.2	5.2	8.4
July					0.3	1.0	1.7	2.6	2.9	3.5	4.1	5.1	8.3
August						0.7	1.5	2.3	2.6	3.2	3.8	4.8	8.0
September							0.8	1.6	1.9	2.5	3.1	4.1	7.3
October								0.9	1.1	1.7	2.3	3.3	6.5
November									0.3	0.8	1.4	2.4	5.6
December										0.6	1.2	2.2	5.3
January 1990											0.6	1.6	4.7
February												1.0	4.1
March													3.0

Car benefit scale rates

CROSS REFERENCES. Benefits in kind; Car fuel scale rates

1990/91	Age of car at end of relevant year of assessment	
	under 4 years £	4 years or more £
Original market value up to £19,250		
(a) with cylinder capacity of		
Up to 1,400 cc	1,700	1,150
1,401 cc to 2,000 cc	2,200	1,500
2,001 cc or more	3,550	2,350
(b) without a cylinder capacity but an original market value of		
Up to £5,999	1,700	1,150
£6,000 to £8,499	2,200	1,500
£8,500 to £19,250	3,550	2,350
Original market value over £19,250		
£19,251 to £29,000	4,600	3,100
£29,001 or more	7,400	4,900

1989/90	under 4 years £	4 years or more £
Original market value up to £19,250		
(a) with cylinder capacity of		
Up to 1,400 cc	1,400	950
1,401 cc to 2,000 cc	1,850	1,250
2,001 cc or more	2,950	1,950
(b) without a cylinder capacity but an original market value of		
Up to £5,999	1,400	950
£6,000 to £8,499	1,850	1,250
£8,500 to £19,250	2,950	1,950
Original market value over £19,250		
£19,251 to £29,000	3,850	2,600
£29,001 or more	6,150	4,100

1988/89	Age of car at end of relevant year of assessment	
	under 4 years £	4 years or more £
Original market value up to £19,250		
(a) with cylinder capacity of		
Up to 1,400 cc	1,050	700
1,401 cc to 2,000 cc	1,400	940
2,001 cc or more	2,200	1,450
(b) without a cylinder capacity but an original market value of		
Up to £5,999	1,050	700
£6,000 to £8,499	1,400	940
£8,500 to £19,250	2,200	1,450
Original market value over £19,250		
£19,251 to £29,000	2,900	1,940
£29,001 or more	4,600	3,060

1987/88	under 4 years £	4 years or more £
Original market value up to £19,250		
(a) with cylinder capacity of		
Up to 1,400 cc	525	350
1,401 cc to 2,000 cc	700	470
2,001 cc or more	1,100	725
(b) without a cylinder capacity but an original market value of		
Up to £5,999	525	350
£6,000 to £8,499	700	470
£8,500 to £19,250	1,100	725
Original market value over £19,250		
£19,251 to £29,000	1,450	970
£29,001 or more	2,300	1,530

Notes

(a) Car benefit scale rates apply to directors and 'P11D' employees (see page 3, note (a)). 'Lower-paid' employees are not taxable in respect of company cars.

(b) Scale rates are reduced for contributions which an employee is required to make for his private use.

(c) For all years, scale charges are proportionally reduced where a car is not available or is incapable of being used for part of a year (being at least 30 days). [ICTA 1988, 6 Sch 2].

(d) The scale charges are reduced by one half where annual business mileage exceeds 17,999 and increased by one half if the car is used for business travel of 2,500 miles or less. [ICTA 1988, 6 Sch 3, 5].

(e) Where any person is taxable in respect of two or more cars, all such cars, other than the one used to the greatest extent for business travel, are charged at one and a half times the appropriate scale rate. This is without prejudice to the increase by one half under (d) above. [ICTA 1988, 6 Sch 5(3)].

Car benefit scale rates (continued)

CROSS REFERENCES. Benefits in kind; Car fuel scale rates

Left columns

1986/87	Age of car at end of relevant year of assessment	
	under 4 years	4 years or more
Original market value up to £19,250	£	£
(a) with cylinder capacity of		
Up to 1,300 cc	450	300
1,301 cc to 1,800 cc	575	380
1,801 cc or more	900	600
(b) without a cylinder capacity but an original market value of		
Up to £5,999	450	300
£6,000 to £8,499	575	380
£8,500 to £19,250	900	600
Original market value over £19,250		
£19,251 to £29,000	1,320	875
£29,001 or more	2,100	1,400

1985/86	under 4 years	4 years or more
Original market value up to £17,500	£	£
(a) with cylinder capacity of		
Up to 1,300 cc	410	275
1,301 cc to 1,800 cc	525	350
1,801 cc or more	825	550
(b) without a cylinder capacity but an original market value of		
Up to £5,499	410	275
£5,500 to £7,699	525	350
£7,700 to £17,500	825	550
Original market value over £17,500		
£17,501 to £26,500	1,200	800
£26,501 or more	1,900	1,270

Right columns

1984/85	Age of car at end of relevant year of assessment	
	under 4 years	4 years or more
Original market value up to £16,000	£	£
(a) with cylinder capacity of		
Up to 1,300 cc	375	250
1,301 cc to 1,800 cc	480	320
1,801 cc or more	750	500
(b) without a cylinder capacity but an original market value of		
Up to £4,949	375	250
£4,950 to £6,999	480	320
£7,000 to £16,000	750	500
Original market value over £16,000		
£16,001 to £24,000	1,100	740
£24,001 or more	1,725	1,150

1983/84	under 4 years	4 years or more
Original market value up to £14,000	£	£
(a) with cylinder capacity of		
Up to 1,300 cc	325	225
1,301 cc to 1,800 cc	425	300
1,801 cc or more	650	450
(b) without a cylinder capacity but an original market value of		
Up to £4,299	325	225
£4,300 to £6,099	425	300
£6,100 to £14,000	650	450
Original market value over £14,000		
£14,001 to £21,000	950	650
£21,001 or more	1,500	1,000

Notes

(a) Car benefit scale rates apply to directors and 'P11D' employees (see page 3, note (a)). 'Lower-paid' employees are not taxable in respect of company cars.

(b) Scale rates are reduced for contributions which an employee is required to make for his private use.

(c) For all years, scale charges are proportionally reduced where a car is not available or is incapable of being used for part of a year (being at least 30 days). [ICTA 1988, 6 Sch 2].

(d) The scale charges are reduced by one half where annual business mileage exceeds 17,999 and increased by one half if the car is used for business travel of 2,500 miles or less. [ICTA 1988, 6 Sch 3, 5].

(e) Where any person is taxable in respect of two or more cars, all such cars, other than the one used to the greatest extent for business travel, are charged at one and a half times the appropriate scale rate. This is without prejudice to the increase by one half under (d) above. [ICTA 1988, 6 Sch 5(3)].

Car fuel scale rates

CROSS REFERENCES. Benefits in kind; Car benefit scale rates

1987/88 to 1990/91	£
Cars with cylinder capacity of	
Up to 1,400 cc	480
1,401 cc to 2,000 cc	600
2,001 cc or more	900
Cars without a cylinder capacity but an original market value of	
Up to £5,999	480
£6,000 to £8,499	600
£8,500 or more	900

1986/87	£
Cars with cylinder capacity of	
Up to 1,300 cc	450
1,301 cc to 1,800 cc	575
1,801 cc or more	900
Cars without a cylinder capacity but an original market value of	
Up to £5,999	450
£6,000 to £8,499	575
£8,500 or more	900

1985/86	£
Cars with cylinder capacity of	
Up to 1,300 cc	410
1,301 cc to 1,800 cc	525
1,801 cc or more	825
Cars without a cylinder capacity but an original market value of	
Up to £5,499	410
£5,500 to £7,699	525
£7,700 or more	825

1984/85	£
Cars with cylinder capacity of	
Up to 1,300 cc	375
1,301 cc to 1,800 cc	480
1,801 cc or more	750
Cars without a cylinder capacity but an original market value of	
Up to £4,949	375
£4,950 to £6,999	480
£7,000 or more	750

1983/84	£
Cars with cylinder capacity of	
Up to 1,300 cc	325
1,301 cc to 1,800 cc	425
1,801 cc or more	650
Cars without a cylinder capacity but an original market value of	
Up to £4,299	325
£4,300 to £6,099	425
£7,000 or more	650

Notes

(a) For 1983/84 and subsequent years, a scale charge applies to directors and higher-paid employees (see page 3 note (a)) provided with free fuel for private use of company cars. [ICTA 1988, s 158].

(b) Scale charges are reduced to nil if the employee is required to make good all fuel provided for private use, including journeys between home and normal place of work. There is no assessable benefit where the employer only provides fuel for business travel. [ICTA 1988, s 158(6)].

(c) Scale charges are proportionally reduced where a car is not available or is incapable of being used for part of a year (being at least 30 days) and are reduced by one half where annual business mileage exceeds 17,999. [ICTA 1988, s 158, 6 Sch 2, 3].

(d) Fuel provided for private motoring of a director or higher-paid employee but not in respect of a company car and fuel provided for lower-paid employees (e.g. by paying garage bills or by use of credit tokens or vouchers) is assessed on the cost to the employer less any contribution from the employee.

Corporation tax rates

CROSS REFERENCES. Interest on overdue tax; Payment of tax

Corporation tax generally

Full rate	1 April 1986 to 31 March 1991		35%	FA 1987, s 21; FA 1988, s 26; FA 1989, s 34; FB 1990

	1 April 1985 to 31 March 1986		40%	
	1 April 1984 to 31 March 1985		45%	
	1 April 1983 to 31 March 1984		50%	FA 1984, s 18(3)

Small companies rate

The small companies rate applies to basic profits (before 17 March 1987, income) of a UK resident company whose profits do not exceed certain limits. The limits and rates are

Period	Limit	Rate	Reference
1 April 1990 to 31 March 1991	£200,000	25%	FB 1990
1 April 1989 to 31 March 1990	£150,000	25%	FA 1989, s 35
1 April 1988 to 31 March 1989	£100,000	25%	FA 1988, s 27
1 April 1987 to 31 March 1988	£100,000	27%	FA 1987, s 22
1 April 1986 to 31 March 1987	£100,000	29%	FA 1986, s 18(1)
1 April 1983 to 31 March 1986	£100,000	30%	FA 1984, s 20(1)

Profits are those on which corporation tax falls finally to be borne plus franked investment income other than from companies within the same group (and for this purpose, distributions are treated as coming from the same group only if dividends so received are group income or would be group income if the companies so elected).

Basic profits are those on which corporation tax falls finally to be borne.

ICTA 1988, s 13(7)
ICTA 1988, s 13(8)

Income is profits on which corporation tax falls finally to be borne, less the amount included in the profit computation in respect of chargeable gains.

FA 1972, ss 85(6), 95(8)

Marginal relief

Where profits of an accounting period exceed the limits for small companies rate above but are less than the 'upper relevant amount' (M), corporation tax is reduced by

$$F(M - \text{profits}) \times \frac{\text{basic profit (before 17 March 1987 income)}}{\text{profits}}$$

where F is a fraction determined by Parliament
Values for M and F are as follows

ICTA 1988, s 13(2)(3)
FA 1972, s 95(2)(3)

Financial year	Values for M	Values for F	
1990	£1,000,000	1/40	FB 1990
1989	£750,000	1/40	FA 1989, s 35
1988	£500,000	1/40	FA 1988, s 27
1987	£500,000	1/50	FA 1987, s 22
1986	£500,000	3/200	FA 1986, s 18(2)
1985	£500,000	1/40	
1984	£500,000	3/80	
1983	£500,000	1/20	FA 1984, s 20(2)

Corporation tax rates (continued)

Marginal relief (continued)	Where an accounting period is less than twelve months, the amounts are proportionately reduced.		*ICTA 1988, s 13(6)*
	Where a company has associated companies, the profit limits for small companies rates and the upper relevant amounts above are divided by one plus the number of associated companies in the accounting period, including those associated for part only of the period but ignoring companies which have not carried on a trade or business at any time in the period.		*ICTA 1988, s 13*
Special rates	(a) Income (excluding capital gains) of building societies, approved housing associations and registered industrial and provident societies (provided they are not controlled by a company or companies outside these categories)		*FA 1972, s 96*
	1 April 1973 to 31 March 1985 (thereafter abolished)	40%	*FA 1974, s 10(3)*
	(b) Income from investments reserved for policyholders of life insurance companies		
	1 April 1973 to 31 March 1986 (thereafter abolished)	37.5%	*ICTA 1970, s 310*
	(c) Income of close investment companies distributing, broadly, less than 85% of total profits		
	1 April 1989 onwards	35%	*FA 1989, s 105*

Corporation tax on chargeable gains

Rate	(a) After 16 March 1987, chargeable gains are taxable at the full rate (or at the small companies rate where profits do not exceed the limits quoted above). Before 17 March 1987, chargeable gains were taxable at the full rate but the gains subject to this rate were reduced by the fractions quoted below (to give an effective rate of 30%). These rules do not apply to authorised unit and investment trusts (see (b) below).		*F(No 2)A 1987, s 74*
	1 April 1986 to 16 March 1987	1/7	
	1 April 1985 to 31 March 1986	1/4	
	1 April 1984 to 31 March 1985	1/3	
	1 April 1983 to 31 March 1984	2/5	*FA 1984, s 18(3)*
	(b) For authorised unit and investment trusts, gains are not chargeable.		*FA 1980, s 81*

Advance corporation tax

Rate	6 April 1988 to 5 April 1991	25/75	
	6 April 1987 to 5 April 1988	27/73	
	6 April 1986 to 5 April 1987	29/71	*ICTA 1988, s 14(3)*
	6 April 1979 to 5 April 1986	3/7	*F(No 2)A 1979, s 6*
			FA 1980, s 20
			FA 1981, s 21
			FA 1982, s 22
			FA 1983, s 12
			FA 1984, s 19
			FA 1985, s 35

Double taxation treaties at 1 May 1990

Agreements covering taxes on income and capital gains (excluding agreements covering shipping and air transport only).

Country	SI or SR & O Number	Country	SI or SR & O Number	Country	SI or SR & O Number
Antigua	**1947 No 2865**	Faroe Islands	**1961 No 579**	Kenya	**1977 No 1299**
	1968 No 1096	(see also Denmark)	1971 No 717	Kiribatu (and Tuvalu)	**1950 No 750**
Aruba (terminated April 1989)	**1970 No 1949★**		1975 No 2190		1968 No 309
Australia	**1968 No 305**	Fiji	**1976 No 1342**		1974 No 1271
	1980 No 707	Finland	**1970 No 153**	Korea	**1978 No 786**
Austria	**1970 No 1947**		1973 No 1327★	Lesotho	**1949 No 2197**
	1979 No 117		1980 No 710		1968 No 1868
Bangladesh	**1980 No 708**		1985 No 1997	Luxembourg	**1968 No 1100**
Barbados	**1970 No 952**	France	**1968 No 1869**		1980 No 567
	1973 No 2096		1971 No 718★		1984 No 364
Belgium	**1987 No 2053**		1973 No 1328	Malawi	**1956 No 619**
	1970 No 636★		1987 No 466		1964 No 1401
Belize	**1947 No 2866**		1987 No 2055		1968 No 1101
	1968 No 573	Gambia	**1980 No 1963**		1979 No 302
	1973 No 2097	Germany,	**1967 No 25**	Malaysia	**1973 No 1330**
Botswana	**1978 No 183**	Federal Republic of	1971 No 874		1987 No 2056
Brunei	**1950 No 1977**	Ghana	**1978 No 785**	Malta	**1962 No 639**
	1968 No 306	Greece	**1954 No 142**		1975 No 426
	1973 No 2098	Grenada	**1949 No 361**	Mauritius	**1981 No 1121**
Bulgaria	**1987 No 2054**		1968 No 1867		1987 No 467
Burma	**1952 No 751**	Guernsey	**1952 No 1215**	Montserrat	**1947 No 2869**
Canada	**1980 No 709**	Hungary	**1978 No 1056**		1968 No 576
	1980 No 780	India	**1981 No 1120**	Namibia	**1962 No 2788**
	1980 No 1528	Indonesia	**1975 No 2191**		1967 No 1490
	1985 No 1996	Irish Republic	**1976 No 2151**	Netherlands	**1980 No 1961**
	1987 No 2071		1976 No 2152		1983 No 1902
China	**1984 No 1826**	Isle of Man	**1955 No 1205**	Netherlands Antilles	1970 No 1949★
Cyprus	**1975 No 425**	Israel	**1963 No 616**	(terminated April 1989)	
	1980 No 1529		1971 No 391	New Zealand	**1984 No 365**
Denmark	**1980 No 1960**	Italy	**1962 No 2787**		1966 No 1020★
Dominica (terminated	1949 No 359★		1973 No 1763		1980 No 1531★
April 1987)	1968 No 1098★	Ivory Coast	**1987 No 169**	Nigeria	**1987 No 2057**
Egypt	**1980 No 1091**	Jamaica	**1973 No 1329**		
Falkland Islands	**1984 No 363**	Japan	**1970 No 1948**		
	1949 No 360★		1980 No 1530		
	1968 No 575★	Jersey	**1952 No 1216**		
	1974 No 2149★				

Double taxation treaties (continued)

Agreements covering taxes on income and capital gains (continued)

Country	SI or SR & O Number
Norway	**1985 No 1998**
	1970 No 154*
	1979 No 118*
	1979 No 303*
	1980 No 711*
	1980 No 712*
	1980 No 1962*
Pakistan	**1987 No 2058**
	1961 No 2467*
Philippines	**1978 No 184**
Poland	**1978 No 282**
Portugal	**1969 No 599**
Rumania	**1977 No 57**
St. Christopher and Nevis	**1947 No 2872**
St. Lucia (terminated April 1988)	1949 No 366*
	1968 No 1102*
St. Vincent (terminated April 1987)	1949 No 367*
	1968 No 1103*
Sierra Leone	**1947 No 2873**
	1968 No 1104
Singapore	**1967 No 483**
	1978 No 787
Solomon Islands	**1950 No 748**
	1968 No 574
	1974 No 1270
South Africa	**1969 No 864**
Spain	**1976 No 1919**
Sri Lanka	**1980 No 713**
Sudan	**1977 No 1719**
Swaziland	**1969 No 380**
Sweden	**1984 No 366**
	1961 No 577*
	1961 No 619*
	1968 No 2034*
	1974 No 558*
	1980 No 1532*

Country	SI or SR & O Number
Switzerland	**1978 No 1408**
	1982 No 714
Thailand	**1981 No 1546**
Trinidad & Tobago	**1983 No 1903**
Tunisia	**1984 No 133**
Turkey	**1988 No 932**
Tuvalu (and Kiribatu)	**1950 No 750**
	1968 No 309
	1974 No 1271
Uganda	**1952 No 1213**
USA	**1980 No 568**
	1980 No 779
USSR	**1986 No 224**
Yugoslavia	**1981 No 1815**
Zambia	**1972 No 1721**
	1981 No 1816
Zimbabwe	**1982 No 1842**

Agreements covering taxes on capital

Country	SI or SR & O Number
Estate duty agreements	
France	**1963 No 1319**
India	**1956 No 998**
Italy	**1968 No 304**
Netherlands	1950 No 1197*
Pakistan	**1957 No 1522**
Sweden	1965 No 509*
Switzerland	**1957 No 426**
Capital transfer and inheritance tax agreements	
Irish Republic	**1978 No 1107**
Netherlands	**1980 No 706**
South Africa	**1979 No 576**
Sweden	**1981 No 840**
	1989 No 986
USA	**1979 No 1454**

Notes

(a) Entries in bold are for main agreements currently in force.

(b) Agreements marked with a (*) are no longer in force but have applied at some time since 6 April 1984.

Flat rate expense allowances

	1982/83 –1986/87	1987/88 –1988/89	1989/90 –1990/91
	£	£	£
Agriculture			
All workers	45	50	50
Aluminium			
Continual casting process operators, de-dimplers, driers, drill punchers, dross unloaders, firemen, furnace operators and their helpers, leaders, mouldmen, pourers, remelt department labourers, roll flatteners	85	90	95
Cable hands, case-makers, labourers, mates, truck drivers and measurers, storekeepers	40	45	45
Apprentices	30	30	35
All other workers	65	70	75
Banks			
Uniformed bank employees	25	25	30
Brass and copper			
All workers	65	70	75
Building			
Joiners and carpenters	75	80	85
Cement workers and roofing felt and asphalt labourers	35	40	40
Labourers and navvies	25	25	30
All other workers	55	60	60
Building material			
Stone masons	55	60	60
Tile makers and labourers	25	25	30
All other workers	35	40	40
Clothing			
Lacemakers, hosiery bleachers, dyers, scourers and knitters, and knitwear bleachers and dyers	30	30	35
All other workers	20	20	25
Constructional engineering			
Blacksmiths and their strikers, burners, caulkers, chippers, drillers, erectors, fitters, holders up, markers off, platers, riggers, riveters, rivet heaters, scaffolders, sheeters, template workers, turners and welders	75	80	85
Banksmen labourers, shophelpers, slewers and straighteners	40	45	45
Apprentices and storekeepers	30	30	35
All other workers	50	55	55

	1982/83 –1986/87	1987/88 –1988/89	1989/90 –1990/91
	£	£	£
Electrical and electricity supply			
Those workers incurring laundry costs only (generally CEGB employees)	15	15	15
All other workers	60	65	70
Engineering			
Pattern makers	80	85	90
Labourers, supervisory and unskilled workers	40	45	45
Apprentices and storekeepers	30	30	35
Motor mechanics in garage repair shops	65	70	75
All other workers	65	70	75
Food			
All workers	25	25	30
Forestry			
All workers	45	50	50
Glass			
All workers	40	45	45
Heating			
Pipe fitters and plumbers	70	75	80
Coverers, laggers, domestic glaziers, heating engineers and their mates	60	65	70
All gas workers and all other workers	45	50	50
Iron and steel			
Day labourers, general labourers, stockmen, timekeepers, warehouse staff and weighmen	40	45	45
Apprentices	30	30	35
All other workers	80	85	90
Iron mining			
Fillers, miners and underground workers	65	70	75
All other workers	50	55	55
Leather			
Curriers (wet workers), fellmongering workers and tanning operatives (wet)	35	40	40
All other workers	25	25	30
Particular engineering			
Pattern makers	80	85	90
All chainmakers—cleaners, galvanisers, tinners and wire drawers in the wire drawing industry—toolmakers in the lockmaking industry	65	70	75

Flat rate expense allowances (continued)

	1982/83 –1986/87	1987/88 –1988/89	1989/90 –1990/91
	£	£	£
Particular engineering (continued)			
Apprentices and storekeepers	30	30	35
All other workers	40	45	45
Police force			
Uniformed police officers (ranks up to and including Chief Inspector)	35	40	40
Precious metals			
All workers	45	50	50
Printing			
The following occupations in the letterpress section: electrical engineers (rotary presses), electro-typers, ink and roller markers, machine minders (rotary), maintenance engineers (rotary presses) and stereotypers	70	75	80
Benchhands (P & B), compositors (Lp), readers (Lp), T & E section wireroom operators, warehousemen (PprBx)	20	20	25
All other workers	45	50	50
Prisons			
Uniformed prison officers	35	40	40
Public service			
Dock and inland waterways:			
Dockers, dredger drivers and hopper steerers	35	40	40
All other workers	25	25	30
Public transport:			
Garage hands (including cleaners)	35	40	40
Conductors and drivers	25	25	30
Quarrying			
All workers	45	50	50
Railways			
All workers except craftsmen	40[c]	50	50
(for craftsmen see the appropriate industry heading)			
Seamen			
Carpenters (passenger liners)	110	120	125
Carpenters (cargo vessels, tankers, coasters and ferries)	85	90	95

	1982/83 –1986/87	1987/88 –1988/89	1989/90 –1990/91
	£	£	£
Seamen (continued)			
Other seamen (passenger liners)	85[d]	—	—
Other seamen (cargo vessels, tankers, coasters and ferries)	55[d]	—	—
Shipyards			
Blacksmiths and their strikers, boilermakers, burners, carpenters, caulkers, drillers, furnacemen (platers), holders up, fitters, platers, plumbers, riveters, sheet iron workers, shipwrights, tubers and welders	75	80	85
Labourers	40	45	45
Apprentices and storekeepers	30	30	35
All other workers	50	55	55
Textiles			
Carders, carding engineers, overlookers (all) and technicians (in spinning mills)	55	60	60
All other workers	40	45	45
Textile prints			
All workers	40	45	45
Vehicles			
Builders, railway wagon etc. repairers, and railway wagon lifters	70	75	80
Railway vehicle painters and letterers, railway wagon etc. builders' and repairers' assistants	40	45	45
All other workers	25	25	30
Wood and furniture			
Carpenters, cabinet makers, joiners, wood carvers and woodcutting machinists	75	80	85
Artificial limb makers (other than in wood), organ builders and packing-case makers	60	65	70
Coopers not providing own tools, labourers, polishers and upholsterers	30	30	35
All other workers	50	55	55

Notes

(a) These allowances for tools and special clothing have been agreed between the Inland Revenue and the relevant trade unions. The rates do not prevent an individual employee from claiming actual expenses. If the employer provides or pays for what is required, the expense is not regarded as 'necessarily incurred', and no deduction is given.

(b) The expressions 'all workers' and 'all other workers' refer only to manual workers and certain other workers who have to bear the cost of upkeep of tools and special clothing. They do not extend to other employees such as office staff.

(c) Increased to £45 for 1986/87 onwards.

(d) The allowances for 'other seamen' were withdrawn for 1984/85 and subsequent years.

Foreign exchange rates (averages for tax year)

CROSS REFERENCES. Foreign exchange rates (averages for calendar year); Foreign exchange rates (at specified dates)

For claims under *ICTA 1988, s 278* and general use

Country	Method of quoting	Currency per £1					
		1984/85	1985/86	1986/87	1987/88	1988/89	1989/90
Algeria	Dinars	6.32	6.80	7.04	8.13	10.80	12.10
Argentina	Pesos (to 14.6.85)	98.8	535				
	Australs (from 15.6.85)		1.13	1.57	4.31	28.36	2,893
Australia	Dollars	1.50	2.00	2.25	2.39	2.19	2.12
Austria	Schillings	26.1	24.9	21.3	20.96	22.81	20.47
Bahrain	Dinars	0.479	0.517	0.562	0.641	0.665	0.672
Barbados	Dollars	2.50	2.77	2.99	3.42	3.54	3.12
Belgium	Francs	75.3	75.3	62.5	62.11	67.95	60.94
Bolivia	Pesos (to 31.12.86)	2,840	—	2,793,000			
	Bolivianos (from 1.1.87)			2.96	3.57	4.36	4.47
Brazil	Cruzeiros (to 28.2.86)	2,800	9,700				
	Cruzados (from 1.3.86 to 19.1.89)		20.2	21.8	80.0	1,159	
	Cruzados (from 23.1.89)					1.74	21.81
Brunei	Dollars						3.12
Burma	Kyats	10.9	10.9	10.6	10.83	11.37	10.29
Canada	Dollars	1.65	1.89	2.05	2.22	2.17	1.92
Chile	Pesos	133	229	292	387.6	440.7	427.8
Colombia	Pesos	131	209	305	429.18	576.35	647.81
Denmark	Kroner	13.5	13.5	11.4	11.39	12.53	11.28
Egypt	Egyptian pounds	1.04	1.14	1.10	2.88	4.12	4.06
Finland	Markkas	7.80	7.96	7.30	7.25	7.48	6.74
France	Francs	11.4	11.3	9.90	10.02	10.98	9.89
Germany (West)	Deutschmarks	3.73	3.71	3.03	2.98	3.25	2.91
Ghana	Cedis	50.0	82.5	168	286.53	398.14	481.52
Greece	Drachmae	150	193	204	229.89	263.25	264.15
Grenada and Windward Isles	E. Caribbean dollars	3.43	3.62	4.03	4.59	4.76	4.40
Guyana	Dollars	4.92	5.69	6.49	15.6	15.84	48.75
Hong Kong	Dollars	9.82	10.7	11.6	13.26	13.755	12.725
Iceland	Kronur	43.00	57.1	60.6	64.94	84.29	97.58
India	Rupees	14.8	16.6	18.9	21.88	25.93	27.13
Indonesia	Rupiahs	1,310	1,540	2,040	2,809	3,039	2,930
Iran	Rials	115	120	114	118.76	122.54	116.16
Iraq	Dinars	0.389	0.428	0.463	0.529	0.579	0.534
Ireland (Republic of)	Punts (Irish Pounds)	1.20	1.20	1.08	1.12	1.21	1.10
Israel	Shekels (to 2.9.85)	431	1,470				
	New Shekels (from 3.9.85)		2.12	2.25	2.7	3.01	3.19

Foreign exchange rates (averages for tax year)—continued

For claims under *ICTA 1988, s 278* and general use

Country	Method of quoting	Currency per £1					
		1984/85	1985/86	1986/87	1987/88	1988/89	1989/90
Italy	Lire	2,300	2,470	2,110	2,174	2,394	2,142
Jamaica	Dollars	5.20	7.62	8.26	9.17	9.50	10.07
Japan	Yen	305	285	238	234.74	229.33	235.64
Jordan	Dinars	0.491	0.523	0.515	0.575	0.802	10.035
Kenya	Kenyan shillings	18.7	22.4	23.9	28.01	32.22	34.85
Kuwait	Dinars	0.381	0.405	0.431	0.474	0.500	0.479
Lebanon	Lebanese pounds	9.57	24.5	69.4	380.23	804.21	851.0
Libya	Libyan dinars	0.376	0.406	0.461	0.495	0.509	0.484
Luxembourg	Francs						60.94
Malawi	Kwachas	1.83	2.36	2.86	3.82	4.58	4.40
Malaysia	Dollars (Ringgit)	2.99	3.39	3.86	4.29	4.73	4.40
Malta	Maltese pounds	0.594	0.605	0.556	0.571	0.590	0.555
Mauritius	Rupees	18.1	20.2	19.5	21.74	24.47	24.48
Mexico	Pesos	255	491	1,090	2,688	4,061	4,290
Netherlands	Guilders (Florins)	4.22	4.18	3.42	3.36	3.66	3.28
New Zealand	Dollars	2.38	2.67	2.81	2.74	2.77	2.75
Nigeria	Naira	1.08	1.27	2.65	7.3	10.32	12.34
Norway	Kroner	10.7	11.1	10.9	11.16	11.78	10.99
Oman (Sultanate of)	Rials	0.438	0.484	0.571	0.654	0.678	0.626
Pakistan	Rupees	17.9	21.7	24.9	29.33	32.76	34.11
Paraguay	Guaranies	312	374	358	568.18	596.98	1,976
Peru	Soles (to 31.12.85)	5,190	15,800				
	Intis (from 1.1.86)		20.1	20.9	32.05	394.37	14,090
Philippines	Pesos	21.3	25.0	29.9	34.4	36.29	34.81
Portugal	Escudos	197	223	218	237.53	266.09	251.04
Qatar	Riyals	5.05	5.00	5.43	6.13	6.42	5.92
Saudi Arabia	Riyals	4.43	5.01	5.56	6.37	6.60	6.10
Sierra Leone	Leones	3.48	7.46	19.3	47.62	63.24	136.98
Singapore	Dollars	2.70	2.99	3.25	3.52	3.47	3.12
South Africa	Rands	2.05	3.05	3.34	3.45	4.29	4.27
Spain (and Balearic Islands)	Pesetas	208	217	202	202.84	208.27	185.85
Sri Lanka	Rupees	32.0	37.4	41.8	50.0	57.32	62.35
Sweden	Kronor	10.7	11.2	10.3	10.56	11.19	10.29
Switzerland	Francs	3.11	3.09	2.51	2.46	2.77	2.57

For claims under *ICTA 1988, s 278* and general use

Country	Method of quoting	Currency per £1					
		1984/85	1985/86	1986/87	1987/88	1988/89	1989/90
Taiwan	New Taiwan dollars	50.1	54.6	54.6	51.55	49.57	42.49
Tanzania	Tanzanian shillings	20.5	23.1	55.2	119.9	207.27	277.07
Thailand	Bahts	30.6	36.5	38.6	42.92	44.475	41.64
Trinidad & Tobago	Dollars	3.05	3.73	5.38	6.13	7.18	6.92
Tunisia	Dinars	1.00	1.07	1.20	1.41	1.59	1.52
Turkey	Lira	502	754	1,050	1,961	3,013	3,730
Uganda	Ugandan Old Shillings (to 17.5.87)	499	1,030	2,020	2,299		
	Ugandan New Shillings (from 18.5.87)				100.7	257.63	500.38
United Arab Emirates	Dirhams	4.67	5.02	5.46	6.25	6.46	5.97
Uruguay	New Pesos	78.5	150	243	416.67	749.33	1,232
USA	Dollars	1.25	1.37	1.49	1.70	1.80	1.63
Venezuela	Bolivares	16.3	20.2	31.4	49.75	63.78	68.20
Windward Islands —see Grenada and Windward Isles							
Zaire Republic	Zaires	48.6	71.6	96.2	202.02	430.94	704.71
Zambia	Kwachas	2.40	4.49	12.3	14.06	15.85	32.78
Zimbabwe	Dollars	1.70	2.22	2.49	2.86	3.365	3.65
European monetary system	European Currency Units				1.44	1.13	1.54	1.38

Notes

(a) The above figures are reproduced from official Inland Revenue lists, with the exception of the EMS figure for 1988/89, where the official Revenue figure was clearly incorrect and has been replaced by a figure supplied by commercial sources.

(b) For countries not shown or rates not quoted, contact should be made with the Public Enquiry Room at Somerset House (tel: 071-438-6420/5).

Foreign exchange rates (averages for calendar year)

CROSS REFERENCES. Foreign exchange rates (averages for tax year); Foreign exchange rates (at specified dates)

For general use

Country	Method of quoting	Currency per £1						
		1983	1984	1985	1986	1987	1988	1989
Algeria	Dinars	7.21	6.62	6.50	6.94	7.63	10.315	11.10
Argentina	Pesos (to 14.6.85)	13.5	65.8	340				
	Australs (from 15.6.85)			1.13	1.35	3.086	16.183	491.63
Australia	Dollars	1.66	1.52	1.83	2.18	2.35	2.28	2.07
Austria	Schillings	27.2	26.6	26.4	22.3	20.66	21.95	21.60
Bahrain	Dinars	0.570	0.510	0.486	0.552	0.617	0.672	0.707
Barbados	Dollars	3.02	2.66	2.59	2.94	3.29	3.59	3.05
Belgium	Francs	77.3	76.9	76.3	65.4	60.98	65.38	64.49
Bolivia	Pesos (to 31.12.86)	116	1,500	—	2,762,000			
	Bolivianos (from 1.1.87)					3.31	4.26	4.03
Brazil	Cruzeiros (to 28.2.86)	763	2,240	7,020	17,000			
	Cruzados (from 1.3.86)				20.5	49.02	460.33	3.99
Brunei	Dollars							3.19
Burma	Kyats	12.2	11.3	10.6	10.8	10.64	11.26	10.20
Canada	Dollars	1.87	1.75	1.75	2.04	2.17	2.19	1.94
Chile	Pesos	117	129	197	279	355.87	440.21	393.66
Columbia	Pesos	118	132	176	282	393.7	532.67	570.27
Denmark	Kroner	13.8	13.8	13.6	11.8	11.194	11.972	11.969
Egypt	Egyptian pounds	1.25	1.10	1.08	1.12	1.93	4.07	3.88
Finland	Markkas	8.41	8.00	7.96	7.41	7.19	7.44	7.02
France	Francs	11.5	11.6	11.5	10.1	9.80	10.51	10.45
Germany (West)	Deutschmarks	3.86	3.79	3.78	3.16	2.94	3.12	3.08
Ghana	Cedis	5.63	47.2	68.9	145	264.55	360.66	443.88
Greece	Drachmae	133	150	179	204	221.24	252.16	265.64
Grenada & Windward Isles	E. Caribbean dollars	4.08	3.65	3.48	3.95	4.41	4.82	4.42
Guyana	Dollars	4.52	5.08	5.40	5.85	13.16	16.05	39.82
Hong Kong	Dollars	10.9	10.4	10.1	11.4	12.74	13.90	12.65
Iceland	Kronur	36.1	42.0	53.5	60.2	63.29	76.56	93.19
India	Rupees	15.2	15.1	15.8	18.3	21.01	24.69	26.43
Indonesia	Rupiahs	1,330	1,370	1,430	1,830	2,688	3,015	2,905
Iran	Rials	130	120	117	115	116.55	122.05	118.07
Iraq	Dinars	0.469	0.415	0.401	0.455	0.508	0.555	0.524
Ireland (Republic of)	Punts (Irish pounds)	1.22	1.23	1.21	1.09	1.10	1.17	1.16
Israel	Shekels (to 2.9.85)	79.3	303	1,140				
	New Shekels (from 3.9.85)			2.11	2.18	2.6	2.85	3.13

For general use Country	Method of quoting	Currency per £1						
		1983	1984	1985	1986	1987	1988	1989
Italy	Lire	2,300	2,340	2,450	2,180	2,119	2,314	2,246
Jamaica	Dollars	3.75	5.05	6.97	8.06	8.93	9.61	9.13
Japan	Yen	358	316	305	246	236.41	226.92	225.64
Jordan	Dinars	0.547	0.510	0.508	0.515	0.552	0.669	0.954
Kenya	Kenyan shillings	19.9	19.1	21.0	23.5	26.6	31.28	33.29
Kuwait	Dinars	0.442	0.401	0.387	0.426	0.457	0.497	0.481
Lebanon	Pounds	6.84	8.55	20.6	46.5	252.53	731.23	813.85
Libya	Dinars	0.448	0.400	0.382	0.448	0.488	0.508	0.4895
Luxembourg	Francs							64.49
Malawi	Kwachas	1.77	1.86	2.16	2.70	3.51	4.51	4.46
Malaysia	Dollars (Ringgit)	3.50	3.11	3.20	3.77	4.12	4.66	4.43
Malta	Maltese pounds	0.653	0.614	0.596	0.568	0.561	0.586	0.569
Mauritius	Rupees	17.6	18.3	19.7	19.6	20.79	23.63	24.60
Mexico	Pesos	229	250	387	885	2,123	4,046	4,069
Netherlands	Guilders (Florins)	4.32	4.29	4.26	3.57	3.31	3.515	3.47
New Zealand	Dollars	2.25	2.32	2.60	2.79	2.75	2.72	2.73
Nigeria	Naira	1.11	1.07	1.20	1.97	6.71	8.49	11.79
Norway	Kroner	11.0	10.9	11.1	10.8	11.01	11.41	11.30
Oman (Sultanate of)	Rials	0.523	0.466	0.466	0.559	0.630	0.686	0.63
Pakistan	Rupees	19.5	18.4	20.2	24.0	28.09	31.83	33.27
Paraguay	Guaranies (to 31.3.89)	190	259	380	351	500.0	570.87	625.03
	Guaranies (from 1.4.89)							1,871
Peru	Soles (to 31.12.85)	2,290	4,370	12,550				
	Intis (from 1.1.86)				20.4	26.04	59.005	10,707
Philippines	Pesos	16.3	21.5	22.8	29.2	32.89	36.42	34.37
Portugal	Escudos	165	195	220	218	230.11	255.93	257.63
Qatar	Riyals	5.51	4.92	4.70	5.32	5.95	6.46	5.96
Saudi Arabia	Riyals	5.23	4.69	4.68	5.43	6.13	6.68	6.12
Sierra Leone	Leones	2.88	3.36	6.63	12.3	51.81	53.55	90.97
Singapore	Dollars	3.20	2.84	2.83	3.19	3.44	3.58	3.19
South Africa	Rands	1.69	1.93	2.81	3.31	3.33	4.045	4.29
Spain (and Balearic Islands)	Pesetas	216	214	219	205	202.02	207.20	193.72
Sri Lanka	Rupees	35.3	33.6	34.7	40.7	47.62	56.31	58.61
Sweden	Kronor	11.6	11.0	11.1	10.4	10.37	10.945	10.60
Switzerland	Francs	3.18	3.13	3.15	2.62	2.44	2.60	2.70

Foreign exchange rates (averages for calendar year)—continued

For general use Country	Method of quoting	Currency per £1						
		1983	1984	1985	1986	1987	1988	1989
Taiwan	Dollars	60.6	53.7	51.4	55.2	52.08	50.94	43.28
Tanzania	Tanzanian shillings	16.3	19.8	22.4	38.6	101.73	180.83	232.82
Thailand	Bahts	34.5	31.2	34.6	38.2	41.67	44.70	41.85
Trinidad	Dollars	3.63	3.25	3.10	5.26	5.88	6.83	6.95
Tunisia	Dinars	0.986	1.01	1.06	1.14	1.36	1.53	1.56
Turkey	Lira	336	483	661	980	1,370	2,516	3,468
Uganda	Ugandan Old shillings (to 17.5.87)	222	442	795	2,020	2,137		
	Ugandan New shillings (from 18.5.87)					98.04	186.98	358.68
United Arab Emirates	Dirhams	5.57	4.97	4.72	5.38	6.54	6.54	6.00
Uruguay	New Pesos	51.6	73.0	125	218	357.14	635.43	973.16
USA	Dollars	1.51	1.33	1.28	1.47	1.63	1.78	1.64
Venezuela	Bolivares	13.6	17.3	17.7	28.9	44.44	59.44	64.65
Windward Islands— see Grenada & Windward Isles								
Zaire	Zaires	13.2	47.8	63.1	87.0	168.63	324.69	604.34
Zambia	Kwachas	1.87	2.34	3.37	10.8	15.77	14.25	21.88
Zimbabwe	Dollars	1.53	1.66	2.08	2.44	2.71	3.225	3.46
European monetary system	European Currency Units				1.49	1.42	1.50	1.42

Notes

(a) The above figures are reproduced from official Inland Revenue lists, with the exception of the EMS figure for 1988, where the official Revenue figure was clearly incorrect and has been replaced by a figure supplied by commercial sources.

(b) For countries not shown or rates not quoted, contact should be made with the Public Enquiry Room at Somerset House (tel: 071-438-6420/5).

Foreign exchange rates (at specified dates)

CROSS REFERENCES. Foreign exchange rates (averages for tax year); Foreign exchange rates (averages for calendar year)

For general use

Country	Method of quoting	Currency per £1							
		31.12.86	31.3.87	31.12.87	31.3.88	31.12.88	31.3.89	31.12.89	31.3.90
Australia	Dollars	2.21	2.29	2.60	2.54	2.12	2.06	2.04	2.18
Austria	Schillings			20.88	21.93	22.555	22.415	19.185	19.605
Belgium	Francs	59.9	59.9	62.11	65.40	67.40	66.85	57.40	57.80
Canada	Dollars	2.04	2.10	2.44	2.33	2.15	2.02	1.87	1.93
Denmark	Kroner	10.9	10.9	11.42	11.93	12.41	12.43	10.61	10.64
France	Francs	9.43	9.62	10.03	10.6	10.96	10.80	9.33	9.35
Germany (West)	Deutschmarks	2.86	2.90	2.96	3.13	3.21	3.20	2.73	2.78
Hong Kong	Dollars	11.4	12.6	14.6	14.7	14.12	13.145	12.58	12.86
Irish Republic	Punts	1.05	1.09	1.12	1.17	1.20	1.20	1.04	1.04
Italy	Lire	1,990	2,060	2,188	2,318	2,362	2,344	2,045	2,048
Japan	Yen	235	234	227.79	234.25	226	223.50	231.75	259.25
Luxembourg	Francs							57.4	57.8
Netherlands	Guilders	3.23	3.27	3.33	3.51	3.62	3.605	3.08	3.13
Norway	Kroner	10.9	10.9	11.70	11.78	11.88	11.61	10.635	10.81
Portugal	Escudos			245.70	255.75	264.50	263.10	241.20	246.00
South Africa	Rands			3.62	3.99	4.30	4.32	4.11	4.37
Spain	Pesetas			202.02	208.33	204.75	199.05	176.00	177.95
Sweden	Kronor	10.0	10.1	10.87	11.09	11.08	10.86	9.985	6.12
Switzerland	Francs	2.39	2.42	2.39	2.58	2.72	2.805	2.49	2.46
USA	Dollars	1.48	1.61	1.88	1.89	1.81	1.69	1.61	1.65

Note

The above figures are reproduced from official Inland Revenue lists.

Income tax allowances and reliefs

CROSS REFERENCE. Income tax rates

	1983/84	1984/85	1985/86	1986/87	1987/88	1988/89	1989/90	1990/91
Basic allowances and reliefs	£	£	£	£	£	£	£	£
Personal allowance	1,785	2,005	2,205	2,335	2,425	2,605	2,785	3,005
Married man's allowance	2,795	3,155	3,455	3,655	3,795	4,095	4,375	—
Wife's earned income relief earnings up to	1,785	2,005	2,205	2,335	2,425	2,605	2,785	—
Married couple's allowance	—	—	—	—	—	—	—	1,720
Additional personal allowance (note a)	1,010	1,150	1,250	1,320	1,370	1,490	1,590	1,720
Persons over 65								
Age allowance								
Single under 80 (75 for 1989/90 and 1990/91)	2,360	2,490	2,690	2,850	2,960	3,180	3,400	3,670
over 80 (75 for 1989/90 and 1990/91)	2,360	2,490	2,690	2,850	3,070	3,310	3,540	3,820
Married man's allowance—under 80 (75 for 1989/90 and 1990/91)	3,755	3,955	4,255	4,505	4,675	5,035	5,385	—
over 80 (75 for 1989/90 and 1990/91)	3,755	3,955	4,255	4,505	4,845	5,205	5,565	—
Married couple's allowance—under 75	—	—	—	—	—	—	—	2,145
over 75	—	—	—	—	—	—	—	2,185
Income limit (allowance reduced by $\frac{2}{3}$ excess up to and including 1988/89; by $\frac{1}{2}$ excess for 1989/90 and 1990/91)	7,600	8,100	8,800	9,400	9,800	10,600	11,400	12,300
Effective maximum income for claim								
Single under 80 (75 for 1989/90 and 1990/91)	8,463	8,828	9,528	10,173	10,603	11,463	12,630	13,630
over 80 (75 for 1989/90 and 1990/91)	8,463	8,828	9,528	10,173	10,768	11,658	12,910	13,930
Married under 80 (75 for 1989/90 and 1990/91)	9,040	9,300	10,000	10,675	11,120	12,010	13,420	14,480
over 80 (75 for 1989/90 and 1990/91)	9,040	9,300	10,000	10,675	11,375	12,265	13,780	14,860
Miscellaneous								
Blind person's allowance	360	360	360	360	540	540	540	1,080
Dependent relative allowance (note b)								
Women claimants other than married women living with their husbands	145	145	145	145	145	—	—	—
Other claimants	100	100	100	100	100	—	—	—
Income limit	1,731	1,802	1,909	2,006	2,054	—	—	—
Housekeeper allowance (note b)	100	100	100	100	100	—	—	—
Services of daughter or son (note b)	55	55	55	55	55	—	—	—
Widow's bereavement allowance	1,010	1,150	1,250	1,320	1,370	1,490	1,590	1,720

Notes

(a) The additional personal allowance is available to a single person (or to a married man whose wife is incapacitated by illness) in respect of one or more children.

(b) Abolished after 5 April 1988.

Income tax—bases of assessment

	Income chargeable	Basis of assessment		Reference
Schedule A	Property income etc.	Profits or gains arising in respect of rents etc. arising in the chargeable period, less allowable deductions. It does not apply to rents from furnished lettings (unless the landlord so elects), yearly interest or mineral rents, royalties etc. In appropriate cases, the Revenue will accept full accounts, made up annually to the same date, as being those for the tax year in which the accounting period ends		*ICTA 1988, s 15(1)* *Revenue pamphlet* *IR 27, paras 101–103*
Schedule D Cases I and II	Profits of trades, professions etc.			*ICTA 1988, ss 60–63*

Schedule D
Cases I and II — Profits of trades, professions etc.

Opening years

1st tax year	Actual basis
2nd tax year	First 12 months' profits
3rd tax year	Normally preceding year basis
	The taxpayer may elect for both the second and third years to be based on actual profits (but not either alone). If the third year is not on preceding year, it will be as the Board decide. [*ICTA 1988, s 60(4)*]

Intermediate years — Preceding year basis

Closing years

Last year but 2	Preceding year basis
Last year but 1	Preceding year basis
Last year	Actual basis
	The Revenue may elect for actual profits in the penultimate and antepenultimate years if, in aggregate, these exceed profits on the preceding year basis

Partnerships

Where, after 19 March 1985, there is a change in the persons carrying on a partnership in circumstances where an election could be, but is not, made for continuation under *ICTA 1988, s 113(2)*, the basis of assessment on the new partnership is

1st tax year	Actual basis
2nd–4th tax years	Actual basis
5th and 6th tax years	Preceding year basis
	The taxpayer may elect for both the fifth and sixth years to be based on actual profits (but not either alone)

Income tax—bases of assessment (continued)

	Income chargeable	Basis of assessment	Reference
Schedule D **Case III**	Interest receivable etc.	**New source**	
		If income first arose on 6 April in the first year of assessment	
		Year 1 — First year's income	
		Year 2 — First year's income with option of taxpayer to substitute second year's income	
		Year 3 — Second year's income	
		If income first arose after 6 April in the first year of assessment	
		Year 1 — First year's income	
		Year 2 — Second year's income	
		Year 3 — Second year's income with option of taxpayer to substitute third year's income	
		Year 4 — Third year's income	
		Intermediate years — Preceding year basis	
		Closing years	
		Last year but 1 — If income arising within the twelve months to 5 April is greater than the assessment for that year, the excess is chargeable by assessment	
		Last year — Actual income from 6 April to date of disposal of source	*ICTA 1988, ss 64, 66, 67*
		No income in last two years of ownership — Taxpayer may claim to be treated as if he had ceased to possess the source in the year in which income last arose (provided not more than eight years before claim)	
		No income for six consecutive years — Taxpayer may claim to be treated as if he had ceased to possess the source at the end of those six years and immediately thereafter acquired it as a new source	

Income tax—bases of assessment (continued)

	Income chargeable	Basis of assessment		Reference
Schedule D				
Cases IV and V	Overseas income	The basis of assessment is the same as Case III above. The following table indicates whether income is assessed on an arising or remittance basis		*ICTA 1988, ss 65–67*

Resident	Ordinarily resident	Domiciled	British subject	Case IV	Case V		
				Securities	Possessions	Trades, etc.	Pensions
No	N/A	N/A	N/A	Exempt	Exempt	Exempt	Exempt
Yes	Yes	Yes	Yes	Arising	Arising	Arising	90% arising (note b)
Yes	No	Yes	Yes	Remittance	Remittance	Remittance	Remittance
Yes	Yes/No	No	Yes	Remittance	Remittance	Remittance	Remittance
Yes	Yes/No	Yes	No	Arising	Arising	Arising	90% arising (note b)
Yes	Yes/No	No	No	Remittance	Remittance	Remittance	Remittance

Notes

(a) Before 1984/85, 25% relief was available on the income arising (i.e. tax liability is on 75% of such income). For 1984/85 the relief was reducd to 12½%. Thereafter it is abolished.

(b) Before 1986/87 only 50% was assessable for certain pensions payable under the law of the Federal Republic of Germany or of Austria for victims of Nazi persecution. For 1986/87 onwards, such pensions are completely exempt.

			Reference
Case VI	Miscellaneous income	Profit arising in the year of assessment	*ICTA 1988, s 69*

	Income chargeable	Basis of assessment		Reference
Schedule E	Emoluments etc.	Case I	Total emoluments	
		Case II	Emoluments from duties performed in the UK	
		Case III	Remittance basis	

The following table indicates under which case emoluments are taxed

Domiciled	Resident	Ordinarily resident	UK employer	Foreign employer	Wholly UK income	Wholly overseas income	Partly UK/partly overseas duties	
							UK duties	Overseas duties
Yes	Yes	Yes	Immaterial	Immaterial	Case I	Case I note (b)	Case I	Case I note (b)
Yes	Yes	No	Immaterial	Immaterial	Case II	Case III	Case II	Case III
Yes	No	Yes/No	Immaterial	Immaterial	Case II	Exempt	Case II	Exempt
No	Yes	Yes	Yes	N/A	Case I	Case I note (b)	Case I	Case I note (b)
No	Yes	Yes	N/A	Yes	Case I note (a)	Case III	Case I note (a)	Case I notes (a) and (b)
No	Yes	No	Yes	N/A	Case II	Case III	Case II	Case III
No	Yes	No	N/A	Yes	Case II note (a)	Case III	Case II note (a)	Case III
No	No	Yes/No	Yes	N/A	Case II	Exempt	Case II	Exempt
No	No	Yes/No	N/A	Yes	Case II note (a)	Exempt	Case II note (a)	Exempt

Notes

(a) From 1976/77 to 1983/84, such foreign emoluments of an employee who was resident in the UK in the year of assessment and was resident in at least 9 out of the preceding 10 years of assessment were subject to a 25% deduction (thereafter nil). From 1976/77 to 1983/84, such foreign emoluments of other employees were subject to a 50% deduction. In 1984/85 to 1986/87 the deduction was only available if the employee had held such an employment in 1984/85 and each subsequent year *and* at some time between 6 April 1983 and 13 March 1984 inclusive (or before 1 August 1984 under an obligation incurred before 14 March 1984). In 1987/88 and 1988/89 the deduction was reduced to 25% subject to the same conditions. Thereafter it is abolished. [*FA 1974, 2 Sch 3; FA 1984, s 30(9)–(12); ICTA 1988, s 192(4)*].

(b) Where such duties are performed in the course of a qualifying period of 365 days or more, emoluments for those duties receive a 100% deduction. Emoluments of such duties so performed for at least 30 qualifying days in any year of assessment were subject to a 25% deduction in the years 1977/78 to 1983/84 and 12½% in 1984/85. Thereafter the deduction is abolished. [*FA 1977, 7 Sch 2; FA 1984, s 30(1); ICTA 1988, s 193(1), 12 Sch*].

(c) In the years 1977/78 to 1983/84, a 25% deduction applied to duties performed wholly outside the UK for an employer non-resident in the UK. Entitlement to the deduction did not require qualifying absence from the UK. The deduction was reduced to 12½% for 1984/85 and thereafter is abolished. [*FA 1977, 7 Sch 3; FA 1984, s 30(1)*].

(d) After 5 April 1989, directors' and employees' bonuses and similar sums are taxable in the year of receipt. [*FA 1989, s 37*].

Income tax rates

CROSS REFERENCES. Interest on overdue tax; Payment of tax

Taxable incomes	Taxable incomes between	Rate	Equal to tax of	Cumulative income	Cumulative tax
£	£		£	£	£
1989/90 and 1990/91					
Basic rate					
First 20,700	0 — 20,700	25%	5,175	20,700	5,175
Higher rate					
Above 20,700	20,701 upwards	40%			
1988/89					
Basic rate					
First 19,300	0 — 19,300	25%	4,825	19,300	4,825
Higher rate					
Above 19,300	19,301 upwards	40%			
1987/88					
Basic rate					
First 17,900	0 — 17,900	27%	4,833	17,900	4,833
Higher rates					
Next 2,500	17,901 — 20,400	40%	1,000	20,400	5,833
Next 5,000	20,401 — 25,400	45%	2,250	25,400	8,083
Next 7,900	25,401 — 33,300	50%	3,950	33,300	12,033
Next 7,900	33,301 — 41,200	55%	4,345	41,200	16,378
Above 41,200	41,201 upwards	60%			
1986/87					
Basic rate					
First 17,200	0 — 17,200	29%	4,988	17,200	4,988
Higher rates					
Next 3,000	17,201 — 20,200	40%	1,200	20,200	6,188
Next 5,200	20,201 — 25,400	45%	2,340	25,400	8,528
Next 7,900	25,401 — 33,300	50%	3,950	33,300	12,478
Next 7,900	33,301 — 41,200	55%	4,345	41,200	16,823
Above 41,200	41,201 upwards	60%			

Income tax rates (continued)

Taxable incomes	Taxable incomes between	Rate	Equal to tax of	Cumulative income	Cumulative tax
£	£		£	£	£
1985/86					
Basic rate					
First 16,200	0 — 16,200	30%	4,860	16,200	4,860
Higher rates					
Next 3,000	16,201 — 19,200	40%	1,200	19,200	6,060
Next 5,200	19,201 — 24,400	45%	2,340	24,400	8,400
Next 7,900	24,401 — 32,300	50%	3,950	32,300	12,350
Next 7,900	32,301 — 40,200	55%	4,345	40,200	16,695
Above 40,200	40,201 upwards	60%			
1984/85					
Basic rate					
First 15,400	0 — 15,400	30%	4,620	15,400	4,620
Higher rates					
Next 2,800	15,401 — 18,200	40%	1,120	18,200	5,740
Next 4,900	18,201 — 23,100	45%	2,205	23,100	7,945
Next 7,500	23,101 — 30,600	50%	3,750	30,600	11,695
Next 7,500	30,601 — 38,100	55%	4,125	38,100	15,820
Above 38,100	38,101 upwards	60%			
1983/84					
Basic rate					
First 14,600	0 — 14,600	30%	4,380	14,600	4,380
Higher rates					
Next 2,600	14,601 — 17,200	40%	1,040	17,200	5,420
Next 4,600	17,201 — 21,800	45%	2,070	21,800	7,490
Next 7,100	21,801 — 28,900	50%	3,550	28,900	11,040
Next 7,100	28,901 — 36,000	55%	3,905	36,000	14,945
Above 36,000	36,001 upwards	60%			

Income tax rates (continued)

Investment income surcharge		Reference	Standard or basic rates of income tax	
1984/85 Abolished		*FA 1984, 7 Sch 1*	1988/89—1990/91	25%
1983/84			1987/88	27%
First £7,100	Nil		1986/87	29%
Above	15%	*F(No 2)A 1983, s 1*	1979/80—1985/86	30%
1982/83			1978/79	33%
First £6,250	Nil		1977/78	34%
Above	15%	*FA 1982, s 20*	1975/76—1976/77	35%
1980/81 and 1981/82			1974/75	33%
First £5,500	Nil		1973/74	30%
Above	15%	*FA 1980, s 18(1)(b)*	1971/72—1972/73	38.75%
1979/80			1965/66—1970/71	41.25%
First £5,000	Nil		1959/60—1964/65	38.75%
Above	15%	*F(No 2)A 1979, s 5(1)(c)*	1955/56—1958/59	42.5%
1978/79			1953/54—1954/55	45%
Elderly			1951/52—1952/53	47.5%
First £2,500	Nil		1946/47—1950/51	45%
Next £500	10%			
Above £3,000	15%			
Other individuals				
First £1,700	Nil			
Next £550	10%			
Above £2,250	15%	*FA 1978, s 13*		

Additional rates on income of discretionary and accumulation trusts

1988/89—1990/91	10%
1987/88	18%
1986/87	16%
1979/80—1985/86	15%
1978/79	12%

Inheritance tax exemptions

CROSS REFERENCE. Inheritance tax rates

Exempt transfer	Limits and conditions		Reference
Lifetime only			
Potentially exempt transfers	Unless provided to the contrary (e.g. gifts with reservation) (a) transfers by individuals after 17 March 1986 to other individuals or to accumulation and maintenance trusts or trusts for the disabled; and (b) certain transfers after 16 March 1987 by an individual into, or on the disposal or termination of an individual's beneficial interest in, interest in possession trusts are potentially exempt transfers. Such transfers made seven years or more before the death of the transferor are exempt transfers		*IHTA 1984, s 3A* *FA 1986, s 101, 19 Sch* *F(No 2)A 1987, s 96, 7 Sch*
Annual gifts	18.3.86 onwards Any shortfall in usage can be carried forward to the next year and added to the allowance for that year only	£3,000 p.a.	*IHTA 1984, s 19*
Gifts in consideration of marriage	Parent of either party to marriage Grandparent or remoter ancestor of either party to marriage; or by one party of marriage to the other Any other person	£5,000 £2,500 £1,000	*IHTA 1984, s 22*
Normal expenditure out of income	Exempt if (a) transfer made out of post-tax income taking one year with another; and (b) transferor left with sufficient income to maintain usual standard of living		*IHTA 1984, s 21*
Small gifts	All gifts to the same person in the same year not exceeding	£250	*IHTA 1984, s 20*
Lifetime and on death			
Charities		Wholly exempt	*IHTA 1984, s 23*
National purposes	Property may be given or bequeathed to any of the bodies listed in the Schedule to the Act (British Museum, National Gallery, local authorities etc.)		*IHTA 1984, s 25, 3 Sch*
Political parties	Wholly exempt for gifts after 14 March 1988. Before 15 March 1988, wholly exempt unless transfer on death or in preceding 12 months when limited to £100,000		*IHTA 1984, s 24* *FA 1988, s 137*
Public benefit	Gifts of eligible property are exempt provided that (a) transfer is to a non-profit-making body; and (b) Treasury approval is obtained		*IHTA 1984, s 26*
Shares to an employee trust by individuals	Exempt if trustees hold, within one year of transfer, over 50% of the ordinary shares and have voting control. Beneficiaries must include most of the employees		*IHTA 1984, s 28*
Spouse	Wholly exempt unless spouse non-UK-domiciled when limit is	£55,000	*IHTA 1984, s 18*

Inheritance tax rates

CROSS REFERENCES. Capital transfer tax rates; Inheritance tax exemptions; Interest on overdue tax; Payment of tax

Transfers on death after 5 April 1990

(a) Tax on transfers

		Cumulative total £	Rate	Equal to tax of £	Cumulative totals	
					Taxable transfers £	Tax thereon £
First	128,000	0–128,000	Nil	Nil	128,000	Nil
Above	128,000		40%			

(b) Grossing-up of specific transfers which do not bear their own tax

Net values £		Tax payable thereon £		Cumulative totals	
				Net values £	Gross equivalent £
	0–128,000	Nil		128,000	128,000
Above	128,000	Nil + ⅔ (66.667%) for each £ over 128,000			

Chargeable lifetime transfers after 5 April 1990

(a) Tax on gross transfers

Gross taxable transfers £		Gross cumulative total £	Rate	Equal to tax of £	Cumulative totals	
					Taxable transfers £	Tax thereon £
First	128,000	0–128,000	Nil	Nil	128,000	Nil
Above	128,000		20%			

(b) Grossing-up of net lifetime transfers

Net values £		Tax payable thereon £		Cumulative totals	
				Net values £	Gross equivalent £
	0–128,000	Nil		128,000	128,000
Above	128,000	Nil + ¼ (25%) for each £ over 128,000			

Transfers on death after 5 April 1989 and before 6 April 1990

(a) Tax on transfers

		Cumulative total £	Rate	Equal to tax of £	Cumulative totals	
					Taxable transfers £	Tax thereon £
First	118,000	0–118,000	Nil	Nil	118,000	Nil
Above	118,000		40%			

(b) Grossing-up of specific transfers which do not bear their own tax

Net values £		Tax payable thereon £		Cumulative totals	
				Net values £	Gross equivalent £
	0–118,000	Nil		118,000	118,000
Above	118,000	Nil + ⅔ (66.667%) for each £ over 118,000			

Chargeable lifetime transfers after 5 April 1989 and before 6 April 1990

(a) Tax on gross transfers

Gross taxable transfers £		Gross cumulative total £	Rate	Equal to tax of £	Cumulative totals	
					Taxable transfers £	Tax thereon £
First	118,000	0–118,000	Nil	Nil	118,000	Nil
Above	118,000		20%			

(b) Grossing-up of net lifetime transfers

Net values £		Tax payable thereon £		Cumulative totals	
				Net values £	Gross equivalent £
	0–118,000	Nil		118,000	118,000
Above	118,000	Nil + ¼ (25%) for each £ over 118,000			

Inheritance tax rates (continued)

CROSS REFERENCES. Capital transfer tax rates; Inheritance tax exemptions; Interest on overdue tax; Payment of tax

Transfers on death after 14 March 1988 and before 6 April 1989

(a) Tax on transfers

		Cumulative total £	Rate	Equal to tax of £	Cumulative totals	
					Taxable transfers £	**Tax thereon** £
First	110,000	0–110,000	Nil	Nil	110,000	Nil
Above	110,000		40%			

(b) Grossing-up of specific transfers which do not bear their own tax

Net values £		Tax payable thereon £	Cumulative totals	
			Net values £	**Gross equivalent** £
	0–110,000	Nil	110,000	110,000
Above	110,000	Nil + ⅔ (66.667%) for each £ over 110,000		

Chargeable lifetime transfers after 14 March 1988 and before 6 April 1989

(a) Tax on gross transfers

Gross taxable transfers £		Gross cumulative total £	Rate	Equal to tax of £	Cumulative totals	
					Taxable transfers £	**Tax thereon** £
First	110,000	0–110,000	Nil	Nil	110,000	Nil
Above	110,000		20%			

(b) Grossing-up of net lifetime transfers

Net values £		Tax payable thereon £	Cumulative totals	
			Net values £	**Gross equivalent** £
	0–110,000	Nil	110,000	110,000
Above	110,000	Nil + ¼ (25%) for each £ over 110,000		

Transfers within seven years of death

Such transfers are charged at the death rates but the tax due is tapered as follows where the transfer is more than three years before death.

Year between transfer and death	Percentage of full tax rate
3–4	80%
4–5	60%
5–6	40%
6–7	20%

CROSS REFERENCES. Capital transfer tax rates; Inheritance tax exemptions; Interest on overdue tax; Payment of tax

Transfers on death after 16 March 1987 and before 15 April 1988

(a) Tax on transfers

		Cumulative total £	Rate	Equal to tax of £	Cumulative totals Taxable transfers £	Tax thereon £
First	90,000	0- 90,000	Nil	Nil	90,000	Nil
Next	50,000	90,001-140,000	30%	15,000	140,000	15,000
Next	80,000	140,001-220,000	40%	32,000	220,000	47,000
Next	110,000	220,001-330,000	50%	55,000	330,000	102,000
Above	330,000		60%			

(b) Grossing-up of specific transfers which do not bear their own tax

Net values £	Tax payable thereon £		Cumulative totals Net values £	Gross equivalent £
0- 90,000	Nil		90,000	90,000
90,001-125,000	Nil +	3/7 (42.857%) for each £ over 90,000	125,000	140,000
125,001-173,000	15,000 +	2/3 (66.667%) for each £ over 125,000	173,000	220,000
173,001-228,000	47,000 +	1 (100%) for each £ over 173,000	228,000	330,000
Above 228,000	102,000 +	3/2 (150%) for each £ over 228,000		

Chargeable lifetime transfers after 16 March 1987 and before 15 March 1988

(a) Tax on gross transfers

Gross taxable transfers £		Gross cumulative total £	Rate	Equal to tax of £	Cumulative totals Taxable transfers £	Tax thereon £
First	90,000	0- 90,000	Nil	Nil	90,000	Nil
Next	50,000	90,001-140,000	15%	7,500	140,000	7,500
Next	80,000	140,001-220,000	20%	16,000	220,000	23,500
Next	110,000	220,001-330,000	25%	27,500	330,000	51,000
Above	330,000		30%			

(b) Grossing-up of net lifetime transfers

Net values £	Tax payable thereon £		Cumulative totals Net values £	Gross equivalent £
0- 90,000	Nil		90,000	90,000
90,001-132,500	Nil +	3/17 (17.647%) for each £ over 90,000	132,500	140,000
132,501-196,500	7,500 +	1/4 (25%) for each £ over 132,500	196,500	220,000
196,501-279,000	23,500 +	1/3 (33.333%) for each £ over 196,500	279,000	330,000
Above 279,000	51,000 +	3/7 (42.857%) for each £ over 279,000		

Transfers within seven years of death

Such transfers are charged at the death rates but the tax due is tapered as follows where the transfer is more than three years before death.

Year between transfer and death	Percentage of full tax rate
3-4	80%
4-5	60%
5-6	40%
6-7	20%

Inheritance tax rates (continued)

CROSS REFERENCES. Capital transfer tax rates; Inheritance tax exemptions; Interest on overdue tax; Payment of tax

Transfers on death after 17 March 1986 and before 17 March 1987

(a) Tax on transfers

		Cumulative total £	Rate	Equal to tax of £	Cumulative totals — Taxable transfers £	Cumulative totals — Tax thereon £
First	71,000	0– 71,000	Nil	Nil	71,000	Nil
Next	24,000	71,001– 95,000	30%	7,200	95,000	7,200
Next	34,000	95,001–129,000	35%	11,900	129,000	19,100
Next	35,000	129,001–164,000	40%	14,000	164,000	33,100
Next	42,000	164,001–206,000	45%	18,900	206,000	52,000
Next	51,000	206,001–257,000	50%	25,500	257,000	77,500
Next	60,000	257,001–317,000	55%	33,000	317,000	110,500
Above	317,000		60%			

(b) Grossing-up of specific transfers which do not bear their own tax

Net values £	Tax payable thereon £	Cumulative totals — Net values £	Cumulative totals — Gross equivalent £
0– 71,000	Nil	71,000	71,000
71,001– 87,800	Nil + 3/7 (42.857%) for each £ over 71,000	87,800	95,000
87,801–109,900	7,200 + 7/13 (53.846%) for each £ over 87,800	109,900	129,000
109,901–130,900	19,100 + 2/3 (66.667%) for each £ over 109,900	130,900	164,000
130,901–154,000	33,100 + 9/11 (81.818%) for each £ over 130,900	154,000	206,000
154,001–179,500	52,000 + 1 (100%) for each £ over 154,900	179,500	257,000
179,501–206,500	77,500 + 11/9 (122.222%) for each £ over 179,500	206,500	317,000
Above 206,500	110,500 + 3/2 (150%) for each £ over 206,500		

Chargeable lifetime transfers after 17 March 1986 and before 17 March 1987

(a) Tax on gross transfers

Gross taxable transfers £	Gross cumulative total £	Rate	Equal to tax of £	Cumulative totals — Taxable transfers £	Cumulative totals — Tax thereon £
First 71,000	0– 71,000	Nil	Nil	71,000	Nil
Next 24,000	71,001– 95,000	15%	3,600	95,000	3,600
Next 34,000	95,001–129,000	17½%	5,950	129,000	9,550
Next 35,000	129,001–164,000	20%	7,000	164,000	16,550
Next 42,000	164,001–206,000	22½%	9,450	206,000	26,000
Next 51,000	206,001–257,000	25%	12,750	257,000	38,750
Next 60,000	257,001–317,000	27½%	16,500	317,000	55,250
Above 317,000		30%			

(b) Grossing-up of net lifetime transfers

Net values £	Tax payable thereon £	Cumulative totals — Net values £	Cumulative totals — Gross equivalent £
0– 71,000	Nil	71,000	71,000
71,001– 91,400	Nil + 3/17 (17.647%) for each £ over 71,000	91,400	95,000
91,401–119,450	3,600 + 7/33 (21.212%) for each £ over 91,400	119,450	129,000
119,451–147,450	9,550 + 1/4 (25%) for each £ over 119,450	147,450	164,000
147,451–180,000	16,550 + 9/31 (29.032%) for each £ over 147,450	180,000	206,000
180,001–218,250	26,000 + 1/3 (33.333%) for each £ over 180,000	218,250	257,000
218,251–261,750	38,750 + 11/29 (37.931%) for each £ over 218,250	261,750	317,000
Above 261,750	55,250 + 3/7 (42.857%) for each £ over 261,750		

Transfers within seven years of death

Such transfers are charged at the death rates but the tax due is tapered as follows where the transfer is more than three years before death.

Year between transfer and death	Percentage of full tax rate
3–4	80%
4–5	60%
5–6	40%
6–7	20%

Inland Revenue explanatory pamphlets

IR 1 (1988)	Extra-Statutory Concessions as at August 1988 (with 1990 Supplement)
IR 4	IT and Pensioners (1988)
IR 4A	IT—Age Allowance (1988)
IR 6	Double Taxation Relief (1984)
IR 9 (1984)	The Tax Treatment of Livestock—The Herd Basis (1985)
IR 12	Occupational Pension Schemes—Notes on approval (1979 with 1987 Supp on free-standing additional voluntary contributions)
IR 13	IT—Wife's Earnings Election (1988)
IR 14/15	Construction Industry Tax Deduction Scheme (1983 with 1989 Supp)
IR 20	Residents and Non-residents—Liability to Tax in the UK (1986)
IR 22	IT—Personal Allowances (1988)
IR 23	IT and Widows (1988)
IR 24	Class 4 NI Contributions (1986)
IR 26	IT Assessments on Business Profits—Changes of Accounting Date (1982)
IR 27	Notes on the Taxation of Income from Real Property (1984)
IR 28	Starting in Business (1988)
IR 29	IT and One-parent Families (1988)
IR 30	IT: Separation and Divorce (1987)
IR 31	IT and Married Couples (1989)
IR 32	IT: Separate Assessment (1988)
IR 33	IT and School Leavers (1988)
IR 34	IT: PAYE (1990)
IR 35	IT: Shares for Employees (1989)
IR 36	Approved Profit-sharing Schemes (1981 with FA 1982 and 1983 Supps)
IR 37	IT and CGT: Appeals (1989)
IR 38	IT: SAYE Share Options (1987)
IR 39	Approved Savings-related Share Option Schemes (1981)
IR 40	IT: Conditions for getting a Sub-contractor's Tax Certificate (1982)
IR 41	IT and the Unemployed (1989)
IR 42	IT: Lay-offs and Short-time Work (1989)
IR 43	IT and Strikes (1989)
IR 45	IT, CGT and CTT: What happens when someone dies (1988)
IR 46	IT and CT: Clubs, Societies and Associations (1982)
IR 51	Business Expansion Scheme (1989)
IR 52	Your Tax Office — why it is where it is (1989)
IR 53	Thinking of Taking Someone on? (1989)
IR 55	Bank Interest—Paying Tax (1985)
IR 56	Employed or Self-employed? (1988)
IR 57	Thinking of Working for Yourself? (1988)
IR 60	IT and Students (1985)
IR 63	MIRAS—Mortgage interest relief at source (1988)
IR 64	Giving to Charity: how businesses can get tax relief (1986)
IR 65	Giving to Charity: how individuals can get tax relief (1990)
IR 66	Stamp Duty (1986)
IR 67	Capital taxation and the National Heritage (1986)
IR 68	Accrued Income Scheme (1987)
IR 69	Expenses: Forms P11D. How to Save Yourself Work (1987)
IR 70	Computerised Payroll (1987)
IR 71	PAYE: Inspection of Employers' and Contractors' records (1990)
IR 72	Inland Revenue Investigations: The examination of Business Accounts (1987)
IR 73	Inland Revenue Investigations: How Settlements are negotiated (1989)
IR 74	Deeds of Covenant: Getting it right for tax (1987 with 1988 Insert)
IR 75	Tax reliefs for Charities (1987)
IR 76	Personal Pension Schemes — Guidance Notes (1988)
IR 77	Taxation of Maintenance Payments (1989)
IR 78	Personal Pensions (1989)
IR 80	Independent Taxation — A guide for Married Couples (1989)
IR 81	Independent Taxation — A guide for Pensioners (1989)
IR 82	Independent Taxation — A guide for Husbands on a Low Income (1989)
IR 83	Independent Taxation — A guide for Tax Practitioners (1990)
IR 84	Have You Anything To Declare? (1989)
IR 85	Business Expansion Scheme — Private Rented Housing (1988)
IR 86	Independent Taxation — A Guide To Mortgage Interest Relief For Married Couples (1989)

Inland Revenue explanatory pamphlets (continued)

IR 89	Personal Equity Plans (PEPs) — A guide for Potential Investors (1989)
IR 90	Independent Taxation — A guide to Tax Allowances and Reliefs (1989)
IR 91	Independent Taxation — A guide for Widows and Widowers (1989)
IR 92	Income Tax — A guide for One-Parent Families (1989)
IR 93	Income Tax — Separation, Divorce and Maintenance Payments (1990)
IR 95	Shares for Employees — Profit-Sharing Schemes (1989)
IR 96	Profit-Sharing Schemes — Explanatory Notes (1989)
IR 97	Shares for Employees —SAYE Share Options (1989)
IR 98	SAYE Share Option Schemes — Explanatory Notes (1989)
IR 99	Shares for Employees — Executive Share Options (1989)
IR 100	Executive Share Option Schemes — Explanatory Notes (1989)
IR 103	Tax Relief for Private Medical Insurance (1990)
IR 104	Simple Tax Accounts (1990)
IR 105	How Your Profits Are Taxed (1990)
IR 106	Capital Allowances for Vehicles and Machinery (1990)
46Q	IT—Returning payments in the entertainment industry (1983)
480	IT—Notes on Expenses Payments and Benefits for Directors and certain Employees (1987)
Miras 6	Mortgage Interest and your Tax Relief (1982)
CA 1	IT and CT—Capital Allowances on Machinery or Plant (1973 with FA 1976 and 1984 Supps)
CA 2	IT and CT—Capital Allowances in Industrial Buildings (1972 with FA 1978 and 1984 Supps)

CA 4	IT and CT—Allowances for Scientific Research (1973)
CGT 4	CGT—Owner-occupied Houses (1989)
CGT 6	Retirement: disposal of a business (1985)
CGT 11	CGT and the Small Business (1990)
CGT 13	Indexation Allowance for Quoted Shares (1989)
CGT 14	Capital Gains Tax — An Introduction (1989)
CGT 15	Capital Gains Tax — A Guide For Married Couples (1989)
CGT 16	Capital Gains Tax — Indexation Allowance; Disposals After 5 April 1988 (1989)

IHT 1	Inheritance Tax (1987 with 1988 Supp)
IHT 3	An Introduction To Inheritance Tax (1989)
PRP 2	Profit-Related Pay: Notes for Guidance (1989)
P 5	Farmer's Guide to PAYE (1985)
P 7	Employer's Guide to PAYE (1989)

—	List of admissible and inadmissible taxes for double taxation relief
—	List of bodies approved by the Inland Revenue under Sec 201
—	Explanatory notes on setting up an approved share option scheme
—	Charities—Payroll Giving Schemes
—	Personal Equity Plan Information Pack

The Board of Inland Revenue also issue Press Releases and Statements of Practice. These are included in *Tolley's Official Tax Statements*.

Interest factor tables

CROSS REFERENCES. Interest on overdue tax; Payment of tax

YEAR	Jan	Feb	Mar	Apr	May	June	July	Aug	Sept	Oct	Nov	Dec	Year
1965	0.840	0.8425	0.845	0.8475	0.850	0.8525	0.855	0.8575	0.860	0.8625	0.865	0.8675	1965
1966	0.870	0.8725	0.875	0.8775	0.880	0.8825	0.885	0.8875	0.890	0.8925	0.895	0.8975	1966
1967	0.900	0.9025	0.905	0.9075	0.910	0.9133	0.9167	0.920	0.9233	0.9267	0.930	0.9333	1967
1968	0.9367	0.940	0.9433	0.9467	0.950	0.9533	0.9567	0.960	0.9633	0.9667	0.970	0.9733	1968
1969	0.9767	0.980	0.9833	0.9867	0.990	0.9933	0.9967	1.0000	1.0033	1.0067	1.010	1.0133	1969
1970	1.0167	1.020	1.0233	1.0267	1.030	1.0333	1.0367	1.040	1.0433	1.0467	1.050	1.0533	1970
1971	1.0567	1.060	1.0633	1.0667	1.070	1.0733	1.0767	1.080	1.0833	1.0867	1.090	1.0933	1971
1972	1.0967	1.100	1.1033	1.1067	1.110	1.1133	1.1167	1.120	1.1233	1.1267	1.130	1.1333	1972
1973	1.1367	1.140	1.1433	1.1467	1.150	1.1533	1.1567	1.160	1.1633	1.1667	1.170	1.1733	1973
1974	1.1767	1.180	1.1833	1.1867	1.190	1.1933	1.197	1.2045	1.212	1.2195	1.227	1.2345	1974
1975	1.242	1.2495	1.257	1.2645	1.272	1.2795	1.287	1.2945	1.302	1.3095	1.317	1.3245	1975
1976	1.332	1.3395	1.347	1.3545	1.362	1.3695	1.377	1.3845	1.392	1.3995	1.407	1.4145	1976
1977	1.422	1.4295	1.437	1.4445	1.452	1.4595	1.467	1.4745	1.482	1.4895	1.497	1.5045	1977
1978	1.512	1.5195	1.527	1.5345	1.542	1.5495	1.557	1.5645	1.572	1.5795	1.587	1.5945	1978
1979	1.602	1.6095	1.617	1.6245	1.632	1.6395	1.647	1.6545	1.662	1.6695	1.677	1.6845	1979
1980	1.692	1.702	1.712	1.722	1.732	1.742	1.752	1.762	1.772	1.782	1.792	1.802	1980
1981	1.812	1.822	1.832	1.842	1.852	1.862	1.872	1.882	1.892	1.902	1.912	1.922	1981
1982	1.932	1.942	1.952	1.962	1.972	1.982	1.992	2.002	2.012	2.022	2.032	2.042	1982
1983	2.0487	2.0553	2.062	2.0687	2.0753	2.082	2.0887	2.0953	2.102	2.1087	2.1153	2.122	1983
1984	2.1287	2.1353	2.142	2.1487	2.1553	2.162	2.1687	2.1753	2.182	2.1887	2.1953	2.202	1984
1985	2.2087	2.2153	2.222	2.2287	2.2353	2.2445	2.2537	2.2628	2.2720	2.2812	2.2903	2.2995	1985
1986	2.3087	2.3178	2.3270	2.3362	2.3453	2.3545	2.3637	2.3728	2.3799	2.3870	2.3940	2.4019	1986
1987	2.4098	2.4178	2.4257	2.4336	2.4411	2.4486	2.4555	2.4624	2.4693	2.4768	2.4843	2.4918	1987
1988	2.4987	2.5056	2.5125	2.5193	2.5262	2.5327	2.5391	2.5456	2.5537	2.5618	2.5708	2.5797	1988
1989	2.5887	2.5983	2.6079	2.6175	2.6271	2.6367	2.6462	2.6564	2.6666	2.6768	2.6871	2.6979	1989
1990	2.7088	2.7196	2.7304	2.7413	2.7521	2.7629	2.7738	2.7846	2.7954	2.8063	2.8171	2.8279	1990

Note

(a) The Inland Revenue have published the interest factor ready-reckoner tables in tax offices to calculate the repayment supplement on overpaid tax and interest on unpaid tax included in investigation settlements. They have issued separate interest tables as at the 5th of each month (repayment supplement) and the 1st of each month (investigation settlements). The tables are, however, the same from 1975 onwards when the repayment supplement was introduced.

(b) The above table takes into account the change in the rate of interest effective from 6 November 1989 (See page 50). In the event of any further changes before December 1990, the factors for the period from the date of change to December 1990 will require amendment.

Interest on overdue tax

CROSS REFERENCES. Interest factor tables; Payment of tax

How to use the table on page 49

1. Work out the difference between the factors for
   (a) the expected date of payment; and
   (b) the normal due date for payment (see page 58).

2. Multiply the tax due by the difference in (1) above.

Rates of interest — general

Period	Rate
1.12.82 – 30.4.85	8%
1.5.85 – 5.8.86	11%
6.8.86 – 5.11.86	8.5%
6.11.86 – 5.4.87	9.5%
6.4.87 – 5.6.87	9%
6.6.87 – 5.9.87	8.25%
6.9.87 – 5.12.87	9%
6.12.87 – 5.5.88	8.25%
6.5.88 – 5.8.88	7.75%
6.8.88 – 5.10.88	9.75%
6.10.88 – 5.1.89	10.75%
6.1.89 – 5.7.89	11.5%
6.7.89 – 5.11.89	12.25%
6.11.89 –	13%

Interest is payable gross and recoverable (as if it were tax charged and due and payable under the assessment to which it relates) as a Crown debt; it is not deductible from profits or income, and is refundable to the extent that tax concerned is subsequently discharged.

The table may also be used for repayment supplement, which is due on repayments of more than £25. The tax repayment due should be multiplied by the difference between the factors for
(a) the end of the month in which the repayment or set-off is due; and
(b) the relevant date, which is 12 months after the end of the year of assessment for which the repayment is due (unless the tax was originally paid after that date in which case the relevant date is the end of the year of assessment in which the tax is paid).

Inheritance tax

Note. The rates of interest for inheritance tax differ from those charged for other taxes, so that the interest factor table on page 49 is not applicable to inheritance tax.

Rates of interest —	Transfers on Death and Potentially Exempt Transfers	All other Transfers
1.1.80 – 30.11.82	9%	12%
1.12.82 – 30.4.85	6%	8%
1.5.85 – 15.12.86	9%	11%
16.12.86 – 5.6.87	8%	8%
6.6.87 – 5.8.88	6%	6%
6.8.88 – 5.10.88	8%	8%
6.10.88 – 5.7.89	9%	9%
6.7.89 –	11%	11%

Interest is payable gross and is not deductible in computing income, profits or losses for tax purposes. It is refundable to the extent that the tax concerned is subsequently cancelled.

Interest on overdue tax (continued)

Interest on overdue tax

CROSS REFERENCES. Interest factor tables; Payment of tax

Period of interest

Capital gains tax, corporation tax (mainstream), Income tax (Schedule A, Schedule D and income taxed at source—higher rate and additional rate)	See Box
Advance corporation tax, Capital transfer tax, Income tax (Schedule E) and Inheritance tax	From due date to date of payment
PAYE *Regulation 29* determinations and subcontractor's (in construction industry) *Regulation 12* assessments, made after 19 April 1988	From 14 days after end of tax year or from 19 April 1988 if later

Box reprinted by kind permission of Halmer Hudson FCA

Box Interest runs from the reckonable date as shown by the box until the date of payment

	Issue + 30 D is on or before DD						Issue + 30 D is after DD but on or before TD			Issue + 30 D is after TD
	Postpone + 30 D is on or before DD			Postpone + 30 D is after DD but on or before TD		Postpone + 30 D is after TD	Postpone + 30 D is on or before TD		Postpone + 30 D is after TD	
	Final tax + 30 D is on or before DD	Final tax + 30 D is after DD but on or before TD	Final tax + 30 D is after TD	Final tax + 30 D is on or before TD	Final tax + 30 D is after TD		Final tax + 30 D is on or before TD	Final tax + 30 D is after TD		
1. No notice of appeal given or notice given but no application is made to postpone tax	DD	DD	DD	DD	DD	DD	Issue + 30 D	Issue + 30 D	Issue + 30 D	Issue + 30 D
2. Notice of appeal is given and application is made to postpone tax										
(i) Non-postponed tax	DD	DD	DD	Postpone + 30 D	Postpone + 30 D	TD	Postpone + 30 D	Postpone + 30 D	TD	Issue + 30 D
(ii) Postponed tax subsequently payable	DD	Final tax + 30 D	TD	Final tax + 30 D	TD	TD	Final tax + 30 D	TD	TD	Issue + 30 D
3. Increase in original tax										
(i) Assessments issued before 31 July 1982 or subsequent assessments with no notice of appeal	DD	Final tax + 30 D	Final tax + 30 D	Final tax + 30 D	Final tax + 30 D	Final tax + 30 D	Final tax + 30 D	Final tax + 30 D	Final tax + 30 D	Final tax + 30 D
(ii) All other assessments	DD	Final tax + 30 D	TD	Final tax + 30 D	TD	TD	Final tax + 30 D	TD	TD	Issue + 30 D

Key

DD	=	Due date (see Payment of tax, page 60)
Issue + 30 D	=	the 30th day after the issue of the assessment
Postpone + 30 D	=	the 30th day after date on which postponed tax is agreed with the Revenue
Final tax + 30 D	=	the 30th day after issue of notice of total tax due

TD = Table date, as follows

Mainstream corporation tax — 6 months after DD

Schedules A and D — 1 July following tax year

Income taxed at source — higher rates and additional rate
1980/81 onwards: 1 June after end of next tax year
1979/80 and earlier: 1 January after end of tax year

Capital gains tax — as income taxed at source

51

Interest rates

London clearing banks

Date	Base rate %	Deposit rate %	Date	Base rate %	Deposit rate %
9 June 1982	12.5	9.5	15 July 1985	12	6.375
14 July	12	9	29 July	11.5	5.875
2 August	11.5	8.5	9 January 1986	12.5	6.5
18 August	11	8	19 March	11.5	5.625
31 August	10.5	7.375	9 April	11	5.25
7 October	10	6.75	21 April	10.5	4.875
14 October	9.5	6	14 October	11	5
5 November	9	5.5	10 March 1987	10.5	4.5
29 November	10.125	6.25	18 March	10	4
12 January 1983	11	8	29 April	9.5	3.5
16 March	10.5	7.5	11 May	9	3
15 April	10	6.75	7 August	10	3.5
15 June	9.5	6	15 August	10	3.75
3 October	9	5.5	26 October	9.5	3.25
7 March 1984	8.875	5.5	5 November	9	3
14 March	8.625	5.375	4 December	8.5	2.75
10 May	9.125	5.75	12 December	8.5	2.5
6 July	10	6.625	2 February 1988	9	3
12 July	12	8.875	17 March	8.5	2.5
9 August	11.5	8.5	11 April	8	2
10 August	11	8	1 May	7.5	2
20 August	10.5	7.375	3 June	8	2
7 November	10	6.75	6 June	8.5	2.375
23 November	9.625	6.25	22 June	9	2.375
11 January 1985	10.5	7.25	28 June	9.5	2.375
14 January	12	8.75	4 July	10	3
28 January	14	11.25	18 July	10.5	3.25
20 March	13.5	10.375	26 August	12	3.5
29 March	13	10	25 November	13	4.1
2 April	13.125	7.50	24 May 1989	14	4.25
12 April	12.875	7.25	5 October	15	4.5
19 April	12.625	7.125			
12 June	12.5	7			

Note

(a) The London clearing banks are Barclays, Lloyds, Midland and National Westminster. Where rates vary between banks, the average has been taken. From 6 April 1985, interest paid by banks to individuals resident in the UK is subject to the composite rate scheme. The rates quoted are therefore net of tax from that date.

National savings

CROSS REFERENCE. Government and public corporation securities

	National Savings Bank Ordinary account	National Savings Bank Investment account	National savings income bonds	National savings capital bonds
Minimum/maximum holding	£5—£10,000 per individual plus interest	£5—£25,000 plus interest (Upper limit £100,000 for investments made before 31 December 1989.)	£2,000—£25,000 in units of £1,000 (Upper limit £100,000 for investments made before 31 December 1989.)	£100 minimum in multiples of £100. No upper limit.
Who may purchase or invest	Individuals (also jointly) and trustees for sole beneficiaries.	Individuals (also jointly) and trustees for sole beneficiaries.	Individuals (also jointly) and trustees for sole beneficiaries.	Individuals (also jointly) and trustees for sole beneficiaries.
Rate of interest etc.	5% p.a. for each complete month £500 held in account provided account is open for whole of 1990. Otherwise 2½% p.a. interest earned on each £1 on deposit for a complete calendar month.	Current rate of interest available from any Post Office. Interest earned on each whole £ for each day held on deposit.	Current rate of interest available from any Post Office. Interest calculated on a daily basis and paid monthly on the 5th day of each month.	Compound interest rate equivalent to 12% p.a. provided bonds held for five years. (Growth in value is 5½% for first year and increases in each of next four years.) No interest earned after five years. Interest not actually paid until end of five-year period.
Tax position	First £70 (£140 joint) of annual interest free of IT.	All interest liable to IT but paid gross.	All interest liable to IT but paid gross.	Interest taxable each year when earned, even though not necessarily received until up to four years later.
Notice of withdrawal	Up to £100 on demand. Over £100, a few days' written notice.	1 month's written notice (no penalties).	3 months' written notice. No loss of interest if held for one year.	3 months' written notice. No interest paid if withdrawn in first year. If withdrawn after one year but before five years, interest paid at rate ranging from 5½% to c.11% compound, depending on length of time for which bond held.
Other features	The 'Regular Customer Account' scheme allows a depositor who has used his account at a 'nominated' office for at least 6 months to withdraw up to £250 there on demand without his savings book being retained. Standing Orders may be paid free of charge from Ordinary Accounts.	The 'Save-by-Post' scheme allows accounts to be opened and transactions conducted by post.	Income can be paid direct into a bank, building society, NSB account or sent by post.	Statement of Value, giving details of interest earned, sent on each anniversary of purchase.

National savings (continued)

CROSS REFERENCE. **Government and public corporation securities**

	Premium savings bonds	Yearly plan	National Savings Certificates 34th issue	National Savings Certificates 4th index-linked issue
Minimum/maximum holding	£100—£10,000 (minimum of £100 per purchase)	£20—£200 per month in multiples of £5	£25—£1,000 in units of £25 (but see below)	£25—£5,000 in units of £25
Who may purchase or invest	Individuals 16 or over. Under 16, by parents, guardians or grandparents.	Individuals and trustees for sole beneficiaries.	Individuals (also jointly) in own name or name of another person, trustees, charities, registered friendly societies and approved voluntary bodies.	
Rate of interest etc.	Bonds offer the chance every month of winning some 175,000 prizes ranging from £50 to £250,000. Also weekly prizes of £100,000, £50,000 and £25,000. Prize fund represents 6.5% p.a. of the total value of eligible bonds.	In first year, interest is currently 5.75% p.a. Certificates then earn interest at 7.75% p.a. for the next 4 years (giving an average return of 7.5% for the 5 years) No interest if payment withdrawn in first year. Reduced interest if withdrawn in years 2 to 5.	A unit costs £25 and reaches £35.89 after 5 years. This is equivalent to a compound interest rate of 7.5% over the full five years.	If cashed in first year sum invested repaid without interest. If subsequently cashed, earn index-linking and extra interest (see below) for each complete month held.
Tax position	Prizes free of IT and CGT.	All returns free of IT and CGT.	Interest and any bonus or other sum payable is free of income tax and capital gains tax.	
Notice of withdrawal	At least 8 clear working days.	Normally 14 working days.	Written application on form obtainable from most Post Offices—normally within 8 working days.	
Other features	There is no time limit for claiming prizes. May be bought by persons resident abroad unless contravenes national law e.g. USA, Republic of Ireland. Not transferable in life or on death. Not eligible for prize draw until held for 3 clear months.	Payments by monthly standing order. Certificates may be held beyond 4 year initial term, earning interest at the general extension rate for savings certificates (see note (a) on page 56).	A further £10,000 may be invested out of the proceeds of other National Savings certificates which have been held for the full five year term. Unlike other purchases, reinvestment certificates earn interest even if withdrawn within 1 year of purchase, the rate being 6% p.a. for every 3 whole months from date of purchase.	Extra interest: Year 1 3.00% Year 2 3.25% Year 3 3.50% Year 4 4.50% Year 5 6.00%

National Savings Certificates — growth in value/yield (recent issues) based on a £25 unit

In year	By	For each	Value at end of year £	Yield for year %	Compound interest %	In year	By	For each	Value at end of year £	Yield for year %	Compound interest %
Thirty-fourth issue (1/7/88 —						**Twenty-seventh issue (5/4/84 — 7/8/84)**					
1	£1.50	12 months	26.50	6.00		4	62p	3 months	32.44	8.28	
2	43p	3 months	28.22	6.49		5	76p	3 months	35.48	9.37	7.25
3	49.5p	3 months	30.20	7.02		**Twenty-sixth issue (15/8/83 — 19/3/84)**					
4	64p	3 months	32.76	8.48		5	89p	3 months	37.17	10.59	8.26
5	78.25p	3 months	35.89	9.55	7.50	**Twenty-fifth issue (17/11/82 — 13/8/83)**					
Thirty-third issue (1/5/87 — 30/6/88)						5	79p	3 months	35.90	9.65	7.51
1	£1.38	12 months	26.38	5.50							
2	39.5p	3 months	27.96	6.00							
3	45.5p	3 months	29.78	6.50							
4	59.5p	3 months	32.16	8.02							
5	72.5p	3 months	35.06	9.03	7.00						
Thirty-second issue (12/11/86 — 10/3/87)											
2	50p	3 months	28.63	7.51							
3	62p	3 months	31.11	8.66							
4	77p	3 months	34.19	9.90							
5	96p	3 months	38.03	11.23	8.75						
Thirty-first issue (26/9/85 — 11/11/86)											
2	44p	3 months	28.20	6.66							
3	55p	3 months	30.40	7.80							
4	68p	3 months	33.12	8.95							
5	84p	3 months	36.48	10.14	7.85						
Thirtieth issue (13/2/85 — 9/9/85)											
3	62p	3 months	31.17	8.64							
4	78p	3 months	34.29	10.01							
5	98p	3 months	38.21	11.43	8.85						
Twenty-ninth issue (15/10/84 — 12/2/85)											
4	69p	3 months	33.34	9.03							
5	85p	3 months	36.74	10.20	8.00						
Twenty-eighth issue (8/8/84 — 11/9/84)											
4	80p	3 months	34.43	10.25							
5	£1.01	3 months	38.47	11.73	9.00						

Notes

(a) The first to sixth issues of National Savings certificates (pre-World War II) may be held indefinitely with interest at constant rates until the Treasury give contrary notice. In all cases, interest yields are below 2% and decreasing annually. For later issues, the Treasury periodically increases the period for which certificates may be held as the original dates expire. From June 1982, a common rate of interest is earned for certificates of the 7th to 14th, 16th, 18th, 19th, 21st, 23rd, 24th and 25th issues as their existing extension periods come to an end. Interest (currently at 5.01% p.a.) will be earned for each complete period of three months.

(b) For details of 2nd index-linked issue and supplements thereon see the 1985/86 edition and for details of the 3rd index-linked issue, see the 1986/87 edition.

(c) Overseas residents should ensure that any proposed investment in National Savings is permitted under the laws of the country where they reside.

(d) Most forms of National Savings can be held in the names of children under the age of seven but withdrawals etc. are not allowed until the child reaches that age, except in special circumstances.

Negligible value securities

UK quoted company	Securities	Date
Acrow plc	25p Ord	1984/85
	Non-voting 25p 'A' Ord	
	8% partly Conv Loan	
	Stk 1992/2002	
	8% Uns Loan Stk	
	1992/2002	
	5½% Cum Prefs of £1	
Alfred Clough plc	20p Ord	1986/87
	9% £1 Cum Prefs	
Allen (WG) and Sons (Tipton) plc	25p Ord	1986/87
	5% £1 Cum Prefs	
Alnery No 152 plc	25p Ord	1983/84
Associated Telecommunications plc	25p Ord	1984/85
Austin (F) (Leyton)	10p Ord	1982/83
	£1 11¾% Part Conv Red Prefs 1994	
Bambers Stores plc	10p Ord	1983/84
Barget plc	25p Ord	1985/86
Bastian International plc	20p Ord	1984/85
Beechwood Group plc	10p Ord	1984/85
Ben Williams & Co Ltd	10p Ord	1984/85
	6% £1 Cum Prefs	
Berwick Timpo plc	25p Ord	1983/84
	5½% £1 Cum Prefs	
Blackwood, Morton & Sons (Holdings)	25p Ord	1982/83
British Anzani plc	5p Ord	1986/87
Brocks (The) Group of Companies	10p Ord	1983/84
Capper-Neill plc	10p Ord	1984/85
Caravans International	20p Ord	1982/83
Carron Co (Holdings)	25p Ord	1982/83
Castle (GB) plc[c]	25p Ord	1986/87
Clark Son & Morland	£1 7% 2nd Cum Prefs	1982/83
Cocksedge (Holdings) plc	25p Ord	1985/86
	9.5% Cum Prefs	
Crouch Group plc	25p Ord	1984/85
Danks Gowerton plc	25p Ord	1986/87
Deanson (Holdings) plc	10p Ord	1984/85

UK quoted company	Securities	Date
Derritron	10p Ord	1982/83
	£1 Prefs	
EC Cases	10p Ord	1985/86
Ellen Road Mill plc	25p Ord	1984/85
Elliot (E) plc	25p Ord	1983/84
Epsley Trust plc	25p Ord	1985/86
	11½% Conv Uns Loan Stock 1988	
Euroflame Holdings plc	20p Ord	1985/86
Findlay Hardware Group	25p Ord	1982/83
	£1 Prefs	
Fraternal Estates	5p Ord	1985/86
Gartons plc	10p Ord	1983/84
	£1 Prefs	
Godwin Warren Control Systems plc	25p Ord	1988/89
Goldman (H) Group plc	10p Ord	1986/87
	9.25% ULS 1982	
Grimshawe Holdings plc	20p Ord	1983/84
Grovebell Group Ltd	5p Ord	1986/87
	£1 Conv Red Cum Prefs	
Herman Smith plc	10p Ord	1985/86
Highgate Optical and Industrial plc	10p Ord	1984/85
ICC Oil Services plc[c]	10p Ord	1986/87
International Property Development	10p Ord	1982/83
James H Dennis & Co Ltd	10p Ord	1984/85
Kentish Property Group plc	5p Ord	1989/90
Lesney Products	5p Ord (Restr Vote)	1982/83
	5p Ord	
	£1 Prefs	
London and Liverpool Trust	10p Ord	1984/85
Maddock plc	20p Ord	1984/85
Mellins plc	5p Ord	1984/85
	25p 10% Cum Prefs	
Melody Mills plc	25p Ord	1982/83
Metro Town and Central Properties	5p Ord	1986/87
Mettoy (The) Company	25p Ord	1984/85
	25p Defd Ord	

UK quoted company	Securities	Date
Midland Industries plc	5p Ord	1984/85
	£1 6% Cum Prefs	
Milbury plc	25p Ord	1985/86
Modern Engineers of Bristol (Holdings) plc	25p Ord	1984/85
Moss (The) Engineering Group	25p Ord	1982/83
Movitex Ltd	10p Ord	1986/87
Northern Developments Holdings plc	10p Ord	Dec 1984
Nova (Jersey) knit	20p Ord	1985/86
Paradise (B) plc	10p Ord	1982/83
Pickles (William)	10p Ord	1983/84
	10p Non Vote Ord	
	£1 5½% Cum Pref	
Pullman (R & J)	5p Ord	1982/83
	20p Prefs	
Rearden Smith Line plc	50p Stock Units	8/8/85
	50p 'A' Non-voting Stock Units	
Rotaprint plc	½p Ord	1988/89
Scotcros plc	25p Ord	1984/85
	6½% £1 Cum Red Prefs	
	6% Unsec Loan Stk 1986/88	
Scotia Investments	10p Ord	1983/84
	12½% Conv Unsec Loan Stk 1976/84 Series A-C	
Scott (David) Group plc	10p Ord	2/3/84
Solex plc	'A' Restr Voting 50p Ord	1985/86
	'B' 50p Ord	

UK quoted company	Securities	Date
Sonic Sound Audio Holdings	10p Ord	1982/83
Sound Diffusion plc	Ord	1988/89
	Pref	
Sparrow Hardwick plc	£1 Ord	1983/84
	£1 Prefs	
Sturla Holdings plc	2p Ord	1984/85
	6½% £1 Cum Prefs	
Thames Investment & Securities plc	£1 Ord	1985/86
	12% 75p Conv Cum Red Prefs	
Tomatin Distillers plc	25p Ord	1984/85
	7% £1 Cum Conv Pref	
Viners plc	1p Ord and 10p Ord	1982/83
	4.9% Conv Red Sec Loan Stock 1988	
Vosper plc	25p Ord	1986/87
	25p Deferred	
W Ribbon Holdings Ltd	10p Ord	1984/85
'W' Ribbons Holdings plc	10p Ord	1986/87
	£1 10% Conv Cum Red Prefs	
Wharf Mill Furnishers	10p Ord	1984/85
Williams Hudson Group	20p Ord	1982/83
	£1 Prefs	
	8½% Conv Uns Loan Stk 1990/95	
	4.5% £1 Cum Prefs	
Wombwell Foundry & Engineering Co Ltd	10p Ord	1982/83
Woodrow Wyatt Holdings plc	5p Ord	1983/84

Notes

(a) The Inland Revenue have accepted that the quoted securities listed above have become of negligible value within the meaning of *CGTA 1979, s 22(2)* with effect from the date or fiscal year given. The securities listed comprise all those company securities in UK quoted companies so accepted after 31 March 1983 and before 1 January 1990.

(b) A list of additional securities accepted by the Inland Revenue as being of negligible value is published quarterly in Tolley's Practical Tax.

(c) These shares were traded on the Unlisted Securities Market.

Payment of tax

	Due date of tax	Reference
Capital gains tax 1980/81 onwards	1 December following tax year★	*FA 1980, s 61(2)*
Capital transfer tax and Inheritance tax (a) lifetime transfers 6 April—30 September 1 October—5 April	30 April in following year Six months after end of month of transfer	*IHTA 1984, s 226(1)*
(b) transfers on death	Six months after end of month in which death occurs or on delivery of account by personal representatives if earlier	*IHTA 1984, s 226(1)(2)*
Corporation tax Accounting periods commencing before 17 March 1987	Nine months after end of accounting period or, for mainstream companies trading since before 1 April 1965, if greater, same interval as there was between end of the basis period of the trade for 1965/66 and 1 January 1966	*ICTA 1970, ss 243, 244*
Accounting periods commencing after 16 March 1987	Nine months after end of accounting period. For mainstream companies trading since before 1 April 1965 the interval above, if greater than nine months, is reduced to nine months in three equal annual steps beginning with the first accounting period starting after 16 March 1987	*FA 1987, s 36* *ICTA 1988, s 10(1)(b)*
Advance corporation tax	Within fourteen days of end of return period during which the qualifying distribution was made. A return period ends on 31 March, 30 June, 30 September, 31 December and at the end of each of the accounting periods	*ICTA 1988, 13 Sch 1, 3*
Income tax Schedule A Schedule B (abolished after 5 April 1988) Schedule D Cases I & II	1 January in tax year★ 1 January in tax year★ One half on 1 January in tax year★ One half on 1 July following end of tax year★	*ICTA 1988, s 5(1)* *ICTA 1988, s 5(1)* *ICTA 1988, s 5(2)(3)*
Case V foreign business other cases Schedule E	As Cases I and II★ 1 January in tax year★ Deductible from emoluments where PAYE is applied or fourteen days after first or, on appeal, revised application by the collector where income is assessed	*ICTA 1988, s 5(1)* *IT (Employments) Regs 1973, Reg 52*
Income taxed at source—higher rate and additional rate 1980/81 onwards	1 December following tax year★	*ICTA 1988, s 5(4)*
Value added tax	Not later than the last day on which the return for the prescribed accounting period must be submitted i.e. for Form VAT 100 not later than one month after the end of the prescribed accounting period	*SI 1985, No 886, Regs 58, 60*

(★) indicates that the due date may be 30 days after issue of the assessment if later.

Personal Pension Schemes

CROSS REFERENCE. Retirement annuity premium limits etc.

Maximum contribution to personal pension	% of Net Relevant earnings		
Age at start of tax year	1988/89	1989/90	1990/91
Under 36	17.5%	17.5%	17.5%
36 to 45	17.5%	20%	20%
46 to 50	17.5%	25%	25%
51 to 55	20%	30%	30%
56 to 60	22.5%	35%	35%
61 and over	27.5%	40%	40%
Maximum relevant earnings	N/A	£60,000	£64,800

Notes

(a) Personal pensions have been available from 1 July 1988.

(b) Where relief is also available for qualifying retirement annuity premiums in a year of assessment, the relief available for personal pension contributions is correspondingly reduced. *ICTA 1988, s 655(1)(a)*

(c) Premiums may be related back to the preceding year of assessment or, if there are no relevant earnings in that year, the last preceding year but one. An election must be made by 5 July following the year of assessment in which payment is made. *ICTA 1988, s 641*

(d) Any unused relief during the past six years can be brought forward and used to cover premiums paid in excess of the normal limit for the year of assessment. *ICTA 1988, s 642*

(e) An individual with relevant earnings from Lloyd's underwriting activities may elect to treat a premium, or part thereof, paid in the year of assessment following that in which a particular underwriting account is closed as having been paid during the year for which the income of that account is assessed. The election must be made by 5 July following the year of payment and only has effect to the extent that the individual has unused relief in the earlier year attributable to the Lloyd's income. *ICTA 1988, s 641*

(f) For approval under *ICTA 1988, s 631*, a contract must normally preclude, inter alia, any payment during the life of the individual other than a life annuity commencing no earlier than age 50 nor later than age 75. The annuity may however be commutable to a lump sum within certain limits. *ICTA 1988, ss 634, 635*

(g) Premiums deductible for contracts under *ICTA 1988, s 637* (lump sum on death before 75) may not exceed 5% of net relevant earnings. *ICTA 1988, s 640(3)*

Remission of tax for official error

After 5 April 1990 (IRPR 20.3.90)

	£	
Normal cases	0–12,000	All
	12,001–14,500	¾
	14,501–18,500	½
	18,501–22,000	¼
	22,001–32,000	$\frac{1}{10}$
	32,001 or more	None
Special cases †	0–15,300	All
	15,301–17,800	¾
	17,801–21,800	½
	21,801–25,300	¼
	25,301–35,300	$\frac{1}{10}$
	35,301 or more	None

After 30 July 1984 and before 23 July 1985 (IRPR 31.7.84)

	£	
Normal cases	0– 8,000	All
	8,001–10,000	¾
	10,001–12,500	½
	12,501–15,000	¼
	15,001–21,500	$\frac{1}{10}$
	21,501 or more	None
Special cases †	0–10,500	All
	10,501–12,500	¾
	12,501–15,000	½
	15,001–17,500	¼
	17,501–24,000	$\frac{1}{10}$
	24,001 or more	None

After 22 July 1985 and before 6 April 1990 (IRPR 23.7.85)

	£	
Normal cases	0– 8,500	All
	8,501–10,500	¾
	10,501–13,500	½
	13,501–16,000	¼
	16,001–23,000	$\frac{1}{10}$
	23,001 or more	None
Special cases †	0–11,000	All
	11,001–13,000	¾
	13,001–16,000	½
	16,001–18,500	¼
	18,501–25,500	$\frac{1}{10}$
	25,501 or more	None

After 21 April 1983 and before 31 July 1984 (IRPR 22.4.83)

	£	
Normal cases	0– 7,500	All
	7,501– 9,500	¾
	9,501–12,000	½
	12,001–14,500	¼
	14,501–20,500	$\frac{1}{10}$
	20,501 or more	None
Special cases †	0– 9,500	All
	9,501–11,500	¾
	11,501–14,000	½
	14,001–16,500	¼
	16,501–22,500	$\frac{1}{10}$
	22,501 or more	None

† Where on the date of the notification the taxpayer is either at least 65 years of age or is in receipt of a national retirement pension or a widow's pension.

Notes

(a) In certain circumstances arrears of tax are wholly or partly waived if they have arisen through the failure of the Inland Revenue to make proper and timely use of information supplied by the taxpayer about his income and personal circumstances. (Inland Revenue ESC A19).

The concession is not normally given where a taxpayer is notified of the arrear by the end of the tax year following that in which it arose.

(b) Inspectors of taxes have discretion to give a measure of relief if the taxpayer's investment income does not represent readily realisable capital (e.g. an annuity) or if his gross income marginally exceeds the limits set out above and he has large or exceptional family responsibilities.

(c) The concession also applies to capital gains tax.

Retail price index

CROSS REFERENCE. Capital gains tax—indexation

Year	Average for year	Jan	Feb	Mar	Apr	May	Jun	Jul	Aug	Sep	Oct	Nov	Dec
1955	11.0	10.7	10.7	10.7	10.8	10.8	11.0	11.0	10.9	11.0	11.2	11.3	11.3
1956	11.5	11.3	11.3	11.4	11.6	11.5	11.5	11.5	11.5	11.5	11.6	11.6	11.6
1957	11.9	11.7	11.7	11.7	11.8	11.8	11.9	12.0	12.0	11.9	12.0	12.1	12.2
1958	12.2	12.2	12.1	12.2	12.3	12.3	12.4	12.2	12.2	12.2	12.3	12.3	12.4
1959	12.3	12.4	12.4	12.4	12.3	12.3	12.3	12.3	12.3	12.2	12.3	12.4	12.4
1960	12.4	12.4	12.4	12.3	12.4	12.4	12.5	12.5	12.4	12.4	12.5	12.6	12.6
1961	12.9	12.6	12.6	12.7	12.8	12.8	12.9	12.9	13.0	13.0	13.0	13.2	13.2
1962	13.4	13.2	13.2	13.3	13.5	13.5	13.6	13.5	13.4	13.4	13.4	13.5	13.5
1963	13.7	13.6	13.7	13.7	13.7	13.7	13.7	13.7	13.6	13.7	13.7	13.7	13.7
1964	14.1	13.8	13.8	13.9	14.0	14.1	14.2	14.2	14.2	14.2	14.3	14.4	14.4
1965	14.8	14.5	14.5	14.5	14.8	14.9	14.9	14.9	14.9	14.9	15.0	15.0	15.1
1966	15.4	15.1	15.1	15.1	15.3	15.4	15.5	15.4	15.5	15.5	15.5	15.6	15.6
1967	15.8	15.7	15.7	15.7	15.8	15.8	15.8	15.7	15.7	15.7	15.8	15.9	16.0
1968	16.5	16.1	16.1	16.2	16.5	16.5	16.3	16.6	16.6	16.6	16.7	16.8	17.0
1969	17.4	17.1	17.2	17.2	17.4	17.4	17.7	17.5	17.4	17.5	17.6	17.6	17.8
1970	18.5	17.9	18.0	18.1	18.4	18.4	18.5	18.6	18.6	18.7	18.9	19.0	19.2
1971	20.3	19.4	19.5	19.7	20.1	20.3	20.4	20.5	20.5	20.6	20.7	20.8	20.9
1972	21.7	21.0	21.1	21.2	21.4	21.5	21.6	21.7	21.9	22.0	22.3	22.4	22.5
1973	23.7	22.6	22.8	22.9	23.3	23.5	23.7	23.8	23.8	24.0	24.5	24.7	24.9
1974	27.5	25.3	25.8	26.0	26.9	27.3	27.6	27.8	27.8	28.1	28.7	29.2	29.6
1975	34.2	30.4	30.9	31.5	32.7	34.1	34.8	35.1	35.3	35.6	36.1	36.6	37.0
1976	39.8	37.5	38.0	38.2	38.9	39.3	39.5	39.6	40.2	40.7	41.4	42.0	42.6
1977	46.1	43.7	44.1	44.6	45.7	46.1	46.5	46.6	46.8	47.1	47.3	47.5	47.8
1978	50.0	48.0	48.3	48.6	49.3	49.6	50.0	50.2	50.5	50.7	51.0	51.3	51.8
1979	56.7	52.5	53.0	53.4	54.3	54.7	55.7	58.1	58.5	59.1	59.7	60.3	60.7
1980	66.8	62.2	63.1	63.9	66.1	66.7	67.4	67.9	68.1	68.5	68.9	69.5	69.9
1981	74.8	70.3	70.9	72.0	74.1	74.6	75.0	75.3	75.9	76.3	77.0	77.8	78.3
1982	81.2	78.7	78.8	79.4	81.0	81.6	81.9	81.9	81.9	81.9	82.3	82.7	82.5
1983	84.9	82.6	83.0	83.1	84.3	84.6	84.8	85.3	85.7	86.1	86.4	86.7	86.9
1984	89.2	86.8	87.2	87.5	88.6	89.0	89.2	89.1	89.9	90.1	90.7	91.0	90.9
1985	94.6	91.2	91.9	92.8	94.8	95.2	95.4	95.2	95.5	95.4	95.6	95.9	96.0
1986	97.8	96.2	96.6	96.7	97.7	97.8	97.8	97.5	97.8	98.3	98.5	99.3	99.6
1987	101.9	100.0	100.4	100.6	101.8	101.9	101.9	101.8	102.1	102.4	102.9	103.4	103.3
1988	106.9	103.3	103.7	104.1	105.8	106.2	106.6	106.7	107.9	108.4	109.5	110.0	110.3
1989	115.2	111.0	111.8	112.3	114.3	115.0	115.4	115.5	115.8	116.6	117.5	118.5	118.8
1990		119.5	120.2	121.4	125.1								

Retirement annuity premium limits etc.

CROSS REFERENCE. **Personal pension schemes**

Age at start of tax year	Overall % limit
1987/88 onwards	
Under 51	17½%
51 to 55	20%
56 to 60	22½%
61 and over	27½%

Year of birth	Overall % limit
1982/83 to 1986/87	
1934 or later	17½%
1916 to 1933	20%
1914 or 1915	21%
1912 or 1913	24%
1910 or 1911	26½%
1908 or 1909	29½%
1907	32½%
1980/81 and 1981/82	
1916 or later	17½%
1914 or 1915	20½%
1912 or 1913	23½%
1910 or 1911	26½%
1908 or 1909	29½%
1907 or earlier	32½%

Notes

(a) Personal pension schemes have been available from 1 July 1988 and it is no longer possible to take out new retirement annuity contracts.

(b) From 1980/81 onwards, any premium paid in a year of assessment can be treated as paid in the last preceding year of assessment or if there are no relevant earnings in that year, the last preceding year but one. An election must be made before the end of the year of assessment in which payment is made or, as regards premiums under contracts made after 30 June 1988, by 5 July following the year of assessment in which payment is made.

ICTA 1988, s 619(4)

(c) From 1980/81, any unused relief during the past six years can be brought forward and used to cover premiums paid in excess of the normal limit for the year of payment.

ICTA 1988, s 625

(d) From 1982/83 onwards, an individual with relevant earnings from Lloyd's underwriting activities may elect to treat a premium, or part thereof, paid in the year of assessment following that in which a particular underwriting account is closed as having been paid during the year for which the income of that account is assessed. The election must be made during the year of payment (or, for contracts made after 30 June 1988, by 5 July following the year of payment) and only has effect to the extent that the individual has unused relief in the earlier year attributable to the Lloyd's income.

ICTA 1988, s 627

(e) For approval under *ICTA 1988, s 620*, a contract must normally preclude, inter alia, any payment during the life of the individual other than a life annuity commencing no earlier than age 60 (50 after 30 June 1988) nor later than age 75. The annuity may however be commutable to a lump sum within certain limits.

ICTA 1988, s 620(2)(3)

(f) Premiums deductible for contracts under *ICTA 1988, s 621* (contracts having as the main object the provision of an annuity for the wife, husband or dependants of the individual or provision of a lump sum on death before 75) may not exceed 5% of net relevant earnings.

ICTA 1988, s 619(3)

(g) The proportion of an annuity paid to a retired partner that can be treated as earned income is calculated by taking 50% of his average share of profits in the best three of the last seven years in which he was a full-time partner. For these purposes, for 1982/83 onwards, the profit share in each of the six years before the year of retirement is uplifted by reference to the increase in the RPI between December in the year in question and December in the year of retirement. The average obtained is also raised yearly by reference to the increase in the RPI between December in the year of retirement and the December preceding the year in which the annuity income is assessed. For values of the RPI, see page 62.

ICTA 1988, s 628

Social security national insurance benefits assessable under Schedule E

CROSS REFERENCE. Social security—taxable and non-taxable state benefits

Weekly rates from weeks commencing	26.11.84	25.11.85	28.7.86	6.4.87	11.4.88	10.4.89	9.4.90
Retirement pensions	£	£	£	£	£	£	£
Married couple—both contributors: each	35.80	38.30	38.70	39.50	41.15	43.60	46.90
—wife non-contributor: joint	57.30	61.30	61.95	63.25	65.90	69.80	75.10
Single person	35.80	38.30	38.70	39.50	41.15	43.60	46.90
Age addition—over 80 (each)	0.25	0.25	0.25	0.25	0.25	0.25	0.25
Widow's benefit (note a)							
Widow's allowance (first 26 weeks of widowhood) (note b)	50.10	53.60	54.20	55.35	57.65	—	—
Widowed mother's allowance (after 26 week period)	35.80	38.30	38.70	39.50	41.15	43.60	46.90
Widow's pension (standard rate) (note c)	35.80	38.30	38.70	39.50	41.15	43.60	46.90
Industrial death benefit (deaths before 11th April 1988 only) (note a)							
Widow's pension (first 26 weeks of widowhood)	50.10	53.60	54.20	55.35	57.65	—	—
Widow's pension (higher permanent rate after 26 weeks)	36.35	38.85	39.25	40.05	41.15	43.60	46.90
Widow's pension (lower permanent rate)	10.74	11.49	11.61	11.85	12.35	13.08	14.07
Old persons' pensions (including age addition) (note d)							
Married couple (both over 80)	34.85	46.50	47.00	48.00	50.00	52.90	56.90
Single person or married man (wife under 80)	21.75	23.25	23.50	24.00	25.00	26.45	28.45
Married woman (husband under 80)	13.10	23.25	23.50	24.00	25.00	26.45	28.45
Unemployment benefit							
Basic	28.45	30.45	30.80	31.45	32.75	34.70	37.35
Increase for adult dependant	17.55	18.80	19.00	19.40	20.20	21.40	23.05
Higher rate where claimant has deferred retirement	35.80	38.30	38.70	39.50	41.15	43.60	46.90
Increase for adult dependant	21.50	23.00	23.25	23.75	24.75	26.20	28.20
Statutory sick pay	varies	varies	varies	varies	varies	varies	varies
Supplementary benefit (means-tested) (note f)	varies	varies	varies	varies	—	—	—
Income support (note f)	—	—	—	—	varies	varies	varies
Invalid care allowance (note a)							
Basic	21.50	23.00	23.25	23.75	24.75	26.20	28.20
Increase for adult dependant	12.85	13.75	13.90	14.20	14.80	15.65	16.85
Invalidity allowances when paid with retirement pensions							
Higher rate	7.50	8.05	8.15	8.30	8.65	9.20	10.00
Middle rate	4.80	5.10	5.20	5.30	5.50	5.80	6.20
Lower rate	2.40	2.55	2.60	2.65	2.75	2.90	3.10

Notes

(a) Exclusive of any addition/allowance paid in respect of a child.

(b) Replaced where husband's death occurs after 10 April 1988 by non-taxable lump sum widow's payment of £1,000.

(c) Reduced rates apply if widow aged below 55 (50 before 11 April 1988) at time of husband's death.

(d) The 'old person's pension' is a non-contributory pension for those over 80. Full details can be found in *Tolley's Social Security and State Benefits*.

(e) Lower rate abolished after 5 October 1985.

(f) Supplementary benefit (before 11 April 1988) and income support (after 10 April 1988) are taxable only in the hands of certain unemployed persons and strikers and then only up to certain limits.

CROSS REFERENCE. Social security—taxable and non-taxable state benefits

Total taxable benefit if received for a full tax year	1984/85	1985/86	1986/87	1987/88	1988/89	1989/90(e)	1990/91
Retirement pensions	£	£	£	£	£	£	£
Married couple—both contributors: each	1,802	1,909	1,991	2,054	2,138	2,264	2,438
—wife non-contributor: joint	2,884	3,056	3,187	3,289	3,424	3,626	3,905
Single person	1,802	1,909	1,991	2,054	2,138	2,264	2,438
Age addition—over 80 (each)	13	13	13	13	13	13	13
Widow's benefit							
Widow's allowance (first 26 weeks of widowhood)	varies	varies	varies	varies	varies	—	—
Widowed mother's allowance (after 26 week period)	1,802	1,909	1,991	2,054	2,138	2,264	2,438
Widow's pension	1,802	1,909	1,991	2,054	2,138	2,264	2,438
Industrial death benefit (deaths before 11th April 1988 only)							
Widow's pension (first 26 weeks of widowhood)	varies	varies	varies	varies	varies	—	—
Widow's pension (higher permanent rate after 26 weeks)	1,830	1,938	2,020	2,083	2,138	2,264	2,438
Widow's pension (lower permanent rate)	540	573	597	616	641	679	731
Old persons' pensions (including age addition)							
Married couple (both over 80)	1,756	2,095	2,418	2,496	2,598	2,748	2,958
Single person or married man (wife under 80)	1,095	1,160	1,209	1,248	1,299	1,374	1,479
Married woman (husband under 80)	660	935	1,209	1,248	1,299	1,374	1,479
Unemployment benefit	varies	varies	varies	varies	varies	varies	varies
Statutory sick pay	varies	varies	varies	varies	varies	—	—
Supplementary benefit/income support	varies	varies	varies	varies	varies	varies	varies
Invalid care allowance							
Basic	1,082	1,146	1,196	1,235	1,286	1,361	1,466
Increase for adult dependant	647	685	715	738	769	813	876
Invalidity allowances when paid with retirement pensions							
Higher rate	378	400	418	432	449	478	520
Middle rate	242	255	265	276	285	301	322
Lower rate	121	128	132	138	143	151	161

Notes

(a) See notes (a) to (e) on previous page.

(b) All figures are exclusive of additional benefits in respect of graduated pension, additional pension etc. which vary with the individual. Certain benefits may be subject to reduction or withdrawal occasioned by any earnings of the individual or of an adult dependant. For retirement pension, if in the five years following pensionable age earnings are above a specified limit, pension received before 1 October 1989 was reduced by half of the first £4 p.w. of any excess and the whole of any further excess. The limits were £75 p.w. from 25.11.85; £70 p.w. from 26.11.84; £65 p.w. from 21.11.83; £57 p.w. from 22.11.82; and £52 p.w. from 12.11.79. Since 30 September 1989 pensions have no longer been reduced in this way.

(c) Retirement pension may be deferred. Subject to conditions, benefit finally payable is increased by 1/7th% for each full week of deferral, subject to a minimum of 7 weeks (1%) and a maximum of 5 years (just over 37%).

(d) The increase effective from 28.7.86 was only taxable in 1986/87 for unemployment benefit, statutory sick pay and supplementary benefit.

(e) FA 1989, s 41 provides that benefits are now assessed on an 'accruals' basis rather than on a receipts basis. Thus, where 53 weekly payments are received in a year, only 52 payments are assessed and one payment escapes tax. This applies to most benefits for 1989/90; the assessable figure is as shown in the above table although this will frequently differ from the amount actually received.

Social security national insurance contributions

Class 1 (earnings related)		1983/84	1984/85	6.4.85–5.10.85	6.10.85–5.4.86	
Lower earnings limit—per week		£32.50	£34.00	£35.50		
—per month		£140.83	£147.33	£153.83		
Upper earnings limit—per week		£235	£250.00	£265.00		
—per month		£1,018.33	£1,083.33	£1,148.33		
Rate of contributions—not contracted out						
Employee %		9	9	9	£35.50—£54.99 pw	5%
					£55—£89.99 pw	7%
					£90—£264.99 pw	9%
					£265 pw and above	£23.85 pw (max)
Employer %		11.95/11.45[a]	11.45/10.45[a]	10.45	£35.50—£54.99 pw	5%
					£55—£89.99 pw	7%
					£90—£129.99 pw	9%
					£130 pw and above	10.45%
Rate of contributions—contracted out						
Employee %	up to lower limit	9	9	9	£35.50—£54.99 pw	5%/2.85%[b]
					£55—£89.99 pw	7%/4.85%[b]
	between lower and upper limit	6.85	6.85	6.85	£90—£264.99 pw	9%/6.85%[b]
					£265 pw and above	£18.92 pw (max)
Employer %	up to lower limit	11.95/11.45[a]	11.45/10.45[a]	10.45	£35.50—£54.99 pw	5%/0.9%[b]
					£55—£89.99 pw	7%/2.9%[b]
	between lower and upper limit	7.85/7.35[a]	7.35/6.35[a]	6.35	£90—£129.99 pw	9%/4.9%[b]
					£130—£264.99 pw	10.45%/6.35%[b]
					£265 pw and above	£18.28 pw + 10.45% of excess over £265 pw
Rate of contributions—women at reduced rate						
Employee %		3.85	3.85	3.85	£35.50—£264.99 pw	3.85%
					£265 pw and above	£10.20 pw (max)

Notes

(a) Before 1985/86, the employer's contribution was supplemented by the National Insurance Surcharge (NIS). In 1983/84, NIS was reduced from 1½% to 1% from 1 August 1983. Different rates applied to local authorities.

In 1984/85 NIS was abolished from 1 October 1984 (6 April 1985 for local authorities).

(b) Higher percentages apply to first £35.50 pw.

Social security national insurance contributions (continued)

Class 1 (earnings related)	1986/87		1987/88	
Not contracted out				
Employee	£38—£59.99 pw	5%	£39—£64.99 pw	5%
	£60—£94.99 pw	7%	£65—£99.99 pw	7%
	£95—£284.99 pw	9%	£100—£294.99 pw	9%
	£285 pw and above	£25.65 pw (max)	£295 pw and above	£26.55 pw (max)
Employer	£38—£59.99 pw	5%	£39—£64.99 pw	5%
	£60—£94.99 pw	7%	£65—£99.99 pw	7%
	£95—£139.99 pw	9%	£100—£149.99 pw	9%
	£140 pw and above	10.45%	£150 pw and above	10.45%
Contracted out				
Employee[a]	£38—£59.99 pw	5%/2.85%	£39—£64.99 pw	5%/2.85%
	£60—£94.99 pw	7%/4.85%	£65—£99.99 pw	7%/4.85%
	£95—£284.99 pw	9%/6.85%	£100—£294.99 pw	9%/6.85%
	£285 pw and above	£20.34 pw (max)	£295 pw and above	£21.05 pw (max)
Employer[a]	£38—£59.99 pw	5%/0.9%	£39—£64.99 pw	5%/0.9%
	£60—£94.99 pw	7%/2.9%	£65—£99.99 pw	7%/2.9%
	£95—£139.99 pw	9%/4.9%	£100—£149.99 pw	9%/4.9%
	£140—£284.99 pw	10.45%/6.35%	£150—£294.99 pw	10.45%/6.35%
	£285 pw and above	£19.65 pw + 10.45% of excess over £285 pw	£295 pw and above	£20.33 pw + 10.45% of excess over £295 pw
Women at reduced rate				
Employee	£38—£284.99 pw	3.85%	£39—£294.99 pw	3.85%
	£285 pw and above	£10.97 pw (max)	£295 pw and above	£11.36 pw (max)

Note

(a) Higher percentages apply to the first £39 pw in 1987/88 (£38 pw in 1986/87).

Class 1 (earnings related)	1988/89		6.4.89—4.10.89	
Not contracted out				
Employee	£41—£69.99 pw	5%	£43—£74.99 pw	5%
	£70—£104.99 pw	7%	£75—£114.99 pw	7%
	£105—£304.99 pw	9%	£115—£325 pw	9%
	£305 pw and above	£27.45 pw (max)	£325 pw and above	£29.25 pw (max)
Employer	£41—£69.99 pw	5%	£43—£74.99 pw	5%
	£70—£104.99 pw	7%	£75—£114.99 pw	7%
	£105—£154.99 pw	9%	£115—£164.99 pw	9%
	£155 pw and above	10.45%	£165 pw and above	10.45%
Contracted out				
Employee[a]	£41—£69.99 pw	5%/3%	£43—£74.99 pw	5%/3%
	£70—£104.99 pw	7%/5%	£75—£114.99 pw	7%/5%
	£105—£304.99 pw	9%/7%	£115—£325 pw	9%/7%
	£305 pw and above	£22.17 pw (max)	£325.01 pw and above	£23.61 pw (max)
Employer[a]	£41—£69.99 pw	5%/1.2%	£43—£74.99 pw	5%/1.2%
	£70—£104.99 pw	7%/3.2%	£75—£114.99 pw	7%/3.2%
	£105—£154.99 pw	9%/5.2%	£115—£164.99 pw	9%/5.2%
	£155—£304.99 pw	10.45%/6.65%	£165—£325 pw	10.45%/6.65%
	£305 pw and above	£21.84 pw + 10.45% of excess over £305 pw	£325.01 pw and above	£23.24 pw + 10.45% of excess over £325 pw
Women at reduced rate				
Employee	£41—£304.99 pw	3.85%	£43—£325 pw	3.85%
	£305 pw and above	£11.74 pw (max)	£325.01 pw and above	£12.51 pw (max)

Note

(a) Higher percentages apply to the first £41 pw for 1988/89 (£43 pw for 1989/90).

Social security national insurance contributions (continued)

Class 1 (earnings related)	5.10.89—5.4.90		1990/91	
Not contracted out Employee	2% on first £43 pw (where earnings exceed £42.99 pw); 9% on earnings between £43 and £325 pw (Where earnings are less than £43 pw, no contributions are payable)		2% on first £46 pw (where earnings exceed £45.99 pw); 9% on earnings between £46 and £350 pw (Where earnings are less than £46 pw, no contributions are payable)	
Employer	£43—£74.99 pw £75—£114.99 pw £115—£164.99 pw £165 pw and above	5% 7% 9% 10.45%	£46—£79.99 pw £80—£124.99 pw £125—£174.99 pw £175 pw and above	5% 7% 9% 10.45%
Contracted out Employee	2% on first £43 pw (where earnings exceed £42.99 pw); 7% on earnings between £43 and £325 pw (Where earnings are less than £43 pw, no contributions are payable)		2% on first £46 pw (where earnings exceed £45.99 pw); 7% on earnings between £46 and £350 pw (Where earnings are less than £46 pw, no contributions are payable)	
Employer[a]	£43—£74.99 pw £75—£114.99 pw £115—£164.99 pw £165—£325 pw £325.01 pw and above	5%/1.2% 7%/3.2% 9%/5.2% 10.45%/6.65% £23.24 pw + 10.45% of excess over £325 pw	£46—£79.99 pw £80—124.99 pw £125—£174.99 pw £175—£350 pw £350.01 pw and above	5%/1.2% 7%/3.2% 9%/5.2% 10.45%/6.65% £25.02 pw + 10.45% of excess over £350 pw
Women at reduced rate Employee	£43—£325 pw £325.01 pw and above	3.85% £12.51 pw (max)	£46—£350 pw £350.01 pw and above	3.85% £13.47 pw (max)

Note

(a) Higher percentages apply to the first £43 pw for 1989/90 (£46 pw for 1990/91).

Class 2 (self-employed, flat rate)	1983/84	1984/85	1985/86	1986/87	1987/88	1988/89	1989/90	1990/91
Small earnings exemption—per year	£1,775	£1,850	£1,925	£2,075	£2,125	£2,250	£2,350	£2,600
Contributions —per week	£4.40	£4.60	£4.75/3.50[a]	£3.75	£3.85	£4.05	£4.25	£4.55
Share fishermen	£7.00	£7.20	£7.55/6.30[a]	£6.55	£6.55	£6.55	£5.80	£6.15
Class 3 (voluntary contributions)								
Contributions —per week	£4.30	£4.50	£4.65/3.40[a]	£3.65	£3.75	£3.95	£4.15	£4.45
Class 4 (self-employed, profits related)								
Lower annual limit	£3,800	£3,950	£4,150	£4,450	£4,590	£4,750	£5,050	£5,450
Upper annual limit	£12,000	£13,000	£13,780	£14,820	£15,340	£15,860	£16,900	£18,200
Percentage rate	6.3%	6.3%	6.3%[b]	6.3%[b]	6.3%[b]	6.3%[b]	6.3%[b]	6.3%[b]
Maximum payable	£516.60	£570.15	£606.69	£653.31	£677.25	£699.93	£746.55	£803.25
Maximum contributions								
Class 1 or Class 1/Class 2 (note (c))	£1,120.95	£1,192.50	£1,264.05	£1,359.45	£1,407.15	£1,454.85	£1,468.98	£1,498.84
Class 4 limiting amount (note (d))	£749.80	£813.95	£824.69	£852.06	£881.30	£914.58	£971.80	£1,044.40

Notes

(a) Higher amount applied for the period 6.4.85 to 5.10.85.

(b) Tax relief is allowed, by deduction from total income, on 50% of Class 4 contributions payable after 5 April 1985.

(c) Where an earner is employed in more than one employment (whether employed earner's employments or self employments) liability for Class 1 or Class 1 and Class 2 contributions cannot exceed the equivalent of 53 primary Class 1 contributions at the maximum standard rate.

(d) Where Class 4 contributions are payable in addition to Class 1 and/or Class 2 contributions, liability for Class 4 contributions cannot exceed such amount as when added to the Class 1 and Class 2 contributions payable (after applying maximum under (c) if appropriate) equals the limiting amount shown above.

Benefits taxable (as earned income under Schedule E)

Income support (from 11 April 1988) (note a)
Industrial death benefit paid as pension (payable in respect of deaths before 11 April 1988 only)
Invalid care allowance
Invalidity allowance when paid with retirement pension
Old person's pension
Retirement pension
Statutory maternity pay
Statutory sick pay
Unemployment benefit (from 5 July 1982)
Widowed mother's allowance
Widow's allowance (see note (b) on page 64)
Widow's pension

Other benefits

Enterprise allowance
Job release allowance (payable to disabled men over 60)

Benefits non-taxable

Main social security benefits

Attendance allowance
Child benefit
Child dependency additions paid with widow's allowance, widowed mother's allowance, retirement pension or invalid care allowance
Child's special allowance (payable only to existing beneficiaries at 11 April 1988)
Guardian's allowance
Invalidity allowance paid other than with basic pension
Invalidity pension (contributory)
Maternity allowance (where statutory maternity pay not available)
Mobility allowance (from 5 April 1982)
One-parent benefit
Severe disablement allowance
Sickness benefit
Widow's payments (from 11 April 1988)

Means-tested benefits

Educational maintenance allowance
Income support (from 11 April 1988 and where not within note (a) below)
Family credit (from 11 April 1988)
Family income supplement (to 10 April 1988)
Hospital patient's travelling expenses
Housing benefit
Uniform and clothing grants for children

Industrial injury benefits

Child allowance paid with industrial death benefit
Disablement benefit, including
    constant attendance allowance
    exceptionally severe disablement allowance
    unemployability supplement
Workmen's compensation supplementation

War pensions

Disablement pension, including
    age allowance
    allowance for lowered standard of occupation
    clothing allowance
    comforts allowance
    constant attendance allowance
    exceptionally severe disablement allowance
    severe disablement occupational allowance
    unemployability allowance
War orphan's pension
War widow's pension

Other benefits

Christmas bonus for pensioners
Employment rehabilitation allowance
Job release allowance (note b)
Job search and employment transfer scheme benefits
School milk and meals
Student grants and scholarships
TOPS training allowances and grants under similar Government schemes for those undergoing training

Notes

(a) Taxable only in the hands of those available for employment or involved in a trade dispute.

(b) Tax-free when paid under a scheme which only permits payment during the last 12 months before state retirement age (60 for a woman, 65 for a man).

(c) The *Social Security Act 1986* implemented a number of reforms to the system of benefits. These were phased in from April 1987 and 1988.

Stamp and capital duties

Annuities
On purchased life and superannuation annuities — 5p per £10 or part

Bearer instruments*
Inland bearer instruments (other than deposit certificates for overseas stock) executed after 26 October 1986 — £1.50 per £100 or part

Overseas bearer instruments (other than deposit certificates for overseas stock or bearer instruments by usage) executed after 26 October 1986 — £1.50 per £100 or part

Inland or overseas deposit certificates for overseas stock or overseas bearer instruments by usage — 10p per £50 or part

Inland or overseas bearer instruments given in substitution for like instruments duly stamped *ad valorem* — 10p

*including all bearer letters of allotment after 24 March 1986, but excluding certain public offers after 1 November 1987 of units comprising shares in both a UK and a foreign company.

Capital duty
On formation of company, issue of share capital and other chargeable transactions of capital companies

Abolished for transactions after 21 March 1988 (Previously £1 per £100 or part)

Conveyance or transfer on sale*
Amount or value of consideration
Not exceeding £500 — 50p per £50 or part
Over £500 — £1 per £100 or part

'Certified transactions', where the amount or value of the consideration is £30,000 or less and the instrument is certified at that figure — Nil

* Instruments executed after 19 March 1984

Demergers
Instruments executed after 24 March 1986 — 50p per £100 or part

Depositary receipts
Conversion of shares into depositary receipts (and transfer into settlement systems)
After 26 October 1986 — £1.50 per £100

Note
See *Tolley's Stamp Duties and Stamp Duty Reserve Tax* for further details of the above charges.

Gifts inter vivos
Instruments executed after 25 March 1985 — Exempt

Government securities — Exempt

Life insurance policies (executed before 1 January 1990)
Policies not exceeding 2 years, maximum duty — 5p
Other policies
Sum assured not more than £50 — Nil
    between £50 and £1,000 — 5p per £100 or part
    over £1,000 — 50p per £1,000 or part

Loan capital (other than loan capital which is short-term, issued and transferred under *Stamp Act 1891, 1 Sch* (Bearer instruments) or issued by certain international organisations)
Instruments executed after 24 March 1986 — 50p per £100 or part

Purchase of own shares
After 26 October 1986 — 50p per £100 or part

Reconstructions and amalgamations
Instruments executed after 24 March 1986 — 50p per £100 or part

Renounceable letters of allotment (unless in respect of stock exempt from stamp duty)
After 26 October 1986 — 50p per £100 or part

Stamp duty reserve tax
After 26 October 1986 — ½%

Stock or marketable securities
Instruments executed in respect of contracts made after 26 October 1986 — 50p per £100 or part
Instruments executed before that date — As conveyance or transfer on sale

Takeovers
Instruments executed after 24 March 1986 — 50p per £100 or part

Unit trust instruments
Instruments executed after 21 March 1988 — Exempt

Voluntary winding-up (transfer of shares on)
Instruments executed after 24 March 1986 — 50p per £100 or part

Uniform allowances

The publishers regret that 1990/91 figures were not available at the time of going to press.

Army	1985/86 £	1986/87 £	1987/88 £	1988/89 £	1989/90 £	1990/91 £
Officers serving at mounted duty with Household Cavalry and the King's Troop RHA	584.03	649.06	680.22	740.58	725.34	
Dismounted officers — colonels and above	394.35	411.45	415.29	404.38	490.26	
Dismounted officers — below colonel	316.73	337.47	353.35	352.85	393.28	

QARANC						
Nursing officers — colonels and above	348.83	381.89	367.76	408.25	396.67	
Nursing officers — below colonel	281.51	305.86	307.53	358.09	382.97	
Non-nursing officers — colonels and above	308.16	350.75	338.72	372.60	381.13	
Non-nursing officers — below colonel	242.33	254.69	270.40	287.77	310.54	

	1985/86	1986/87	1987/88	1988/89	1989/90	1990/91
WRAC women officers — colonels and above	311.79	329.90	311.60	343.24	352.80	
WRAC women officers — below colonel	243.09	264.94	253.88	305.63	309.23	
RAMC and RAOC officers — colonels and above	311.32	336.51	344.76	379.66	369.55	
RAMC and RAOC officers — below colonel	281.91	309.99	321.16	377.21	389.12	

	1985/86	1986/87	1987/88	1988/89	1989/90	1990/91
Male officers SSVC, SLSC	108.24	112.24	119.36	92.71	104.67	
Women officers SSVC	73.82	89.00	85.61	104.05	101.19	

Royal Air Force	1985/86	1986/87	1987/88	1988/89	1989/90	1990/91
Air officers	256.52	275.20	288.27	299.09	315.96	
Group captains	248.69	264.88	277.77	288.27	304.56	
Wing commanders and below	230.75	245.47	257.84	268.84	287.88	

PMRAFNS						
Air officers	254.43	272.91	282.62	287.30	319.44	
Group captains	247.81	255.72	261.92	265.82	297.00	
Wing commanders and below	243.10	250.92	256.91	260.82	291.48	

WRAF						
Air officers	229.56	262.49	254.91	261.04	279.84	
Group captains	217.48	246.54	246.56	252.38	270.72	
Wing commanders and below	208.58	215.55	220.42	225.24	242.40	

Royal Navy and Royal Marines	1985/86	1986/87	1987/88	1988/89	1989/90	1990/91
Officers flag and equivalent ranks	626.43	701.52	728.40	694.32	782.88	
Officers below flag rank	479.60	538.92	570.12	556.56	630.72	
WRNS officers	301.41	335.88	340.08	298.44	331.44	

	1985/86	1986/87	1987/88	1988/89	1989/90	1990/91
Womens medical and dental officers	338.92	336.00	347.04	306.84	345.48	
QARNNS officers (female) — chief nursing officer and above	476.76	512.28	352.20	437.52	465.24	
QARNNS officers (female) — below chief nursing officer	586.76	656.20	662.76	677.40	681.96	
QARNNS officers (male) — chief nursing officer and above	312.92	348.48	352.20	332.04	387.84	
QARNNS officers (male) — below chief nursing officer	289.28	329.64	324.84	300.72	354.60	

Value added tax

Rate	18/6/79 onwards	15%	*F(No 2)A 1979, s 1*

Registration
after 19 March 1990

A person who makes taxable supplies but is not registered is liable to be registered
(a) after the end of any month if the value of taxable supplies in the past 12 months has exceeded the limit in Column A below; or
(b) at any time if there are reasonable grounds for believing that the value of taxable supplies in the next 30 days will exceed the limit in Column A below

VATA 1983, 1 Sch 1
FB 1990

Effective date	Column A
	£
20 March 1990	25,400
15 March 1989	23,600
16 March 1988	22,100
15 May 1987	21,300

Budget Resolution 1990/10
SI 1989/471
SI 1988/508

Deregistration
after 31 May 1990

A registered taxable person who makes taxable supplies ceases to be liable to be registered if, at any time, C & E are satisfied that the value of taxable supplies in the period of one year then beginning will not exceed the limit in Column A below

VATA 1983, 1 Sch 2
FA 1987, s 14(3)

Effective date	Column A
	£
1 June 1990	24,400
1 June 1989	22,600
1 June 1988	21,100
15 May 1987	20,300

SI 1990/682
SI 1989/471
SI 1988 /508

except that a person does not cease to be liable to be registered if C & E are satisfied that the reason the value of taxable supplies will not exceed the limit is that in the period in question he will cease making taxable supplies or will suspend making them for a period of 30 days or more

Partial exemption
after 31 March 1987

Where in any prescribed accounting period or in any longer period the exempt input tax of a taxable person is less than (a) £100 per month on average; or (b) both £250 per month on average *and* 50% of all input tax; or (c) both £500 per month on average *and* 25% of all input tax, all such input tax in the period is treated as attributable to taxable supplies and recoverable in full subject to the normal rules

SI 1985/886
SI 1987/510

Note

Different registration and deregistration rules applied before 20 March 1990. See the 1989/90 edition for details of these.

Value added tax: car fuel scale rates

1987/88 to 1990/91

Quarterly returns	Scale charge £	VAT due per vehicle £
Business travel below 4,500 miles in return period		
Up to 1,400 cc	120	15.65
1,401 cc to 2,000 cc	150	19.56
Over 2,000 cc	225	29.34
Business travel 4,500 miles or over in return period		
Up to 1,400 cc	60	7.82
1,401 cc to 2,000 cc	75	9.78
Over 2,000 cc	113	14.73

Monthly returns	Scale charge £	VAT due per vehicle £
Business travel below 1,500 miles in return period		
Up to 1,400 cc	40	5.21
1,401 cc to 2,000 cc	50	6.52
Over 2,000 cc	75	9.78
Business travel 1,500 miles or over in return period		
Up to 1,400 cc	20	2.60
1,401 cc to 2,000 cc	25	3.26
Over 2,000 cc	38	4.95

Notes

(a) Subject to (d) below, for prescribed accounting periods beginning after 6 April 1987, a taxable person is required to account for output tax where fuel is supplied for private motoring to either himself or his employees. [FA 1986, s 9, 6 Sch]. The scale charges set out above represent the tax-inclusive value of the fuel supplied and apply separately to supplies to each individual in any prescribed accounting period in respect of any one vehicle.

(b) The rules apply to all cars but not to other vehicles such as vans, motor-cycles and invalid cars. They do not apply to pooled cars or cars used exclusively for business purposes. Travel between home and work is regarded as a private rather than business journey.

(c) Where the above scale rates are used, a taxable person can reclaim input tax on all fuel purchased, even if used for private motoring.

(d) A taxable person need not use the above scale charges where there is an element of private motoring provided he does not reclaim input tax on any fuel purchased, whether used for business or private purposes.

700		The VAT guide (1987) (with amendments Nos 1 and 2)
	1/90	Should I be registered for VAT?
	2/83	Registration for VAT — Group treatment
	3/87	Registration for VAT: Corporate bodies organised in divisions
	4/87	Overseas traders and UK VAT
	5/85	Hire purchase and conditional sale: repossessions and transfers of agreements
	7/81	Business promotion schemes
	8/84	Returnable containers
	9/87	Transfer of a business as a going concern
	10/84	Processing and repair of goods and supplies of exchange units
	11/90	Should I cancel my registration?
	12/90	Filling in your VAT return
	13/90	VAT publications
	14/86	Video cassette films: rental and part-exchange
	15/90	The Ins and Outs of VAT
	17/83	Funded pension schemes
	18/86	Relief from VAT on bad debts
	21/90	Keeping records and accounts
	22/89	Admissions
	24/88	Delivery charges
	25/84	Taxis and hire-cars
	26/90	Visits by VAT officers
	28/85	Services supplied by estate agents
	30/89	Default surcharge appeals
	31/86	Pawnbrokers: disposal of pledged goods
	33/87	MSC training programmes and schemes to assist the unemployed
	34/88	Supplies of staff, including directors, etc.
	35/88	Business gifts
	36/88	Dealer loader promotional schemes
	40/88	Persistent misdeclaration penalty
	41/88	Late registration — penalties and reasonable excuse
	42/88	Serious misdeclaration penalty
	43/88	Default interest
	1/77/VMG	Barristers and advocates: tax point on ceasing to practise
701		
	1/87	Charities
	5/86	Clubs and associations — liability to VAT
	6/86	Donated medical and scientific equipment etc.
	7/86	Aids for handicapped persons (with amendment No 1)
	8/85	Postage stamps and philatelic supplies
	9/85	Terminal markets: dealing with commodities (with amendment No 1)
	10/85	Liability of printed and similar matter
	12/89	Sales of antiques, works of art etc. from stately homes
	13/89	Gaming and amusement machines
	14/89	Food
	15/87	Animal feeding stuffs
	16/85	Sewerage services and water
	19/87	Fuel and power
	20/89	Caravans and houseboats
	21/87	Gold and gold coins (with amendment No 1)
	22/84	Tools for the manufacture of goods for export
	23/89	Protective boots and helmets
	24/84	Parking facilities (with amendment No 1)
	25/86	Pet food
	26/84	Betting and gaming
	27/90	Bingo
	28/84	Lotteries
	29/85	Finance
	30/87	Education
	31/88	Health (with amendment No 1)
	32/85	Burial and cremation
	33/89	Trade unions, professional associations and learned societies
	34/89	Competitions in sport and physical recreation
	35/84	Youth clubs
	36/86	Insurance (with amendments Nos 1 and 2)
	37/84	Live animals
	38/89	Seeds and plants
	39/89	VAT liability law
	40/84	Abattoirs
	41/90	Sponsorship
702		Imports and warehoused goods (1988)
	1/88	Importing goods on which VAT has already been paid in the European Community
	3/89	Repayment of import VAT to shipping agents and freight forwarders
	4/89	Importing computer software
	5/89	Mares temporarily exported for covering abroad: reimportation with or without foals at foot

Value added tax: C & E notices (continued)

703		Exports (1987)
	1/89	Freight containers supplied for export
	2/87	Sailaway boats supplied for export
	3/87	VAT-free purchases of sailaway boats
704		Retail exports (1985 with amendment No 5)
	1/85	VAT refunds for visitors to the UK (with amendment No 4)
	2/87	VAT refunds for UK residents going abroad and crews of ships and aircraft (with amendment No 3)
705		Personal exports of new motor cars (1986 with amendment No 1)
706		Partial exemption (1990)
	1/89	Self supply of stationery
	2/90	Capital goods scheme: input tax on computers, land and buildings acquired for use in your business
708		
	1/85	Protected buildings (listed buildings and scheduled monuments) (with amendments Nos 1 and 2)
	2/89	Construction industry
	4/90	Construction: VAT certificates for residential and charity buildings
	SHP/10	Charities and other bodies engaged in new building projects on a self-build or self-help basis
709		
	1/87	Industrial, staff and public sector catering
	2/87	Catering and take-away food
	3/90	Hotels and holiday accommodation
	4/88	Package holidays and other holiday services
	5/88	Tour operators' margin scheme
710		
	1/83	Theatrical agents and Nett Acts
	2/83	Agencies providing nurses and nursing auxiliaries
	3/83	Private investigators: Expenses charged to clients
711		Second-hand cars (1990)
	1/84	VAT and the second-hand car scheme

712		Second-hand works of art, antiques and collectors' pieces (1990)
	2/85	VAT and second-hand works of art, antiques and collectors' pieces
713		Second-hand motor-cycles (1990)
714		Young children's clothing and footwear (1986 with amendment No 2)
717		Second-hand caravans and motor-caravans (1990)
719		VAT refunds for DIY builders (1990)
720		Second-hand boats and outboard motors (1985 with amendment No 1)
721		Second-hand aircraft (1985 with amendment No 1)
722		Second-hand electronic organs (1985 with amendments Nos 1 and 2)
723		Refunds of VAT in the European Community and other countries (1988)
724		Second-hand firearms (1985 with amendments Nos 1 and 2)
726		Second-hand horses and ponies (1985 with amendments Nos 1 and 2)
727		Retail schemes (1987 with amendment No 1)
	1/87	Retail florists—accounting for VAT on Interflora and Teleflorist transactions
	6/87	Choosing your retail scheme
	7/87 to 15/87	How to work Schemes A—J
731		Cash accounting (1987 with amendments Nos 1 and 2)
732		Annual accounting (1988)
741		International services (with amendments Nos 1 and 2)
742		
	1/90	Letting of facilities for sport and physical recreation
	2/90	Sporting rights
742A		Property Development (1990)
742B		Property Ownership (1990)
744		Passenger transport, international freight, ships and aircraft (1984 with amendment No 1)
748		Extra-statutory concessions (1987 with amendment No 1)
749		Local Authorities and similar bodies (1986)

Entries printed in bold type are main subject headings

Index (continued)